RISE ABOVE THE COMPETITION WITH

RISE ABOVE THE COMPETITION WITH

The *Etiquette* Advantage

RULES
FOR THE
BUSINESS
PROFESSIONAL

June Hines Moore

BROADMAN
& HOLMAN
PUBLISHERS

Nashville, Tennessee

10-digit ISBN: 0805401547
13-digit ISBN: 9780805401547

Published by Broadman & Holman Publishers,
Nashville, Tennessee

Illustration on page 139, used by permisson from Dorothea Johnson,
who operates the Protocol School in Washington.

Dewey Decimal Classification: 395.5
Subject Heading: BUSINESS ETIQUETTE/BUSINESS COMMUNICATION
Library of Congress Card Catalog Number: 97-52205

Library of Congress Cataloging-in-Publication Data

Moore, June Hines.
    The etiquette advantage : rules for the business professional / June Hines
Moore.
        p.   cm.
    Includes index.
    ISBN 0-8054-0154-7 (pbk.)
    1. Business etiquette.   2. Business communication.   3. Body language.
I. Title.
HF5389.M66   1998
395.5'2–dc21   97-52205
                                                                          CIP

7 8 9 10 11 12 13 14 15   10 09 08 07 06 05

*To my father, J. D. Hines, who gave me a
strong work ethic;
to my mother, Dorothy Rooks Hines, who
gave me a love for books;
to my family, a gift from God;
and as always, to my husband, Homer, the
most honorable businessman I know.*

Etiquette rules are in our head.

Manners are in our heart.

Together they give us a two-way shield

against embarrassment.

TABLE OF CONTENTS

INTRODUCTION

One of the troubles in the world
today is that we have allowed the Golden Rule
to become a bit tarnished.
Martin Vanbee

Good manners are cost effective because "everyone is watching everybody else's manners, especially in the workplace," according to *The Wall Street Journal, Fortune* magazine, The National Institute of Business Management, and other business publications.[1]

By definition, business etiquette is a set of rules that allow us to communicate and interact in a civilized manner. These arbitrary rules involve the rites and mores, forms and manners that are required in a society or profession. Successful business people usually conform to this expected behavioral code.

A *US News and World Report* survey reveals that a vast majority of Americans feel their country has reached an ill-mannered watershed. Nine out of ten Americans think incivility is a serious problem.

More than 90 percent believe it contributes to the increase of violence in the country. The word *civility* is derived from the Latin *civis*, or citizen, and is also foreshadowed in the word *civitas*, or the art of government.[2]

The rules are fairly simple to keep with minimal effort required, yet the benefits may be considerable. Generally, we prefer no surprises when we transact business because it makes matters less complicated.

Good manners mean good business because they increase the quality of life in the workplace, contribute to employee morale, embellish the company image, and even generate profit. Bright, well-trained employees with klutsy behavior often don't realize when they offend someone and then wonder why they were passed over for promotion.

Since the '60s we have seen a burst of upward mobility taking place. Unfortunately, children who may have rebelled against their parents' training are now earning top grades at business schools but don't know how to handle themselves properly—at business functions in the office, in a public forum, or in a nice restaurant.

The TV-tray generation has missed a lot. Families used to have to pause and talk together. There was an acknowledgment of each other's daily activities, moods, and growth. Now they go to family therapy where the therapist plays the role of the dinner table. It is no wonder that the "separate tables" generation is so focused on "self" and is so wary of manners.

Many of us have become addicted to the pleasures of a selfish society with its emphasis on individual expression, the flouting of convention, and the free vent of emotions.

Yet, if I know the rules and adapt them to the manners in my heart, I won't embarrass myself or anyone else. For instance, once I was in a CEO's office discussing a workshop for his company. He said, "Mrs. Moore, we surely do need a lot of 'et-a-kwet' taught today."

I used to teach French and English and now I teach "e-ti-ket," a good English word borrowed from the French. You can imagine how much I wanted to correct him, but the manners in my heart stopped me. My embarrassing him would have been far worse than his mis-pronunciation of the word, "etiquette."

Etiquette is not a code worked up to serve the purpose of class distinction. The rules have reasons, such as the following:

- We use napkins because they are an improvement over wiping our hands on the tablecloth.
- We place the knife and fork next to each other on the plate when we have finished eating because they are less likely to drop off when the plate is taken away.
- We dress up to show respect.

Through experience with the way manners have been taught, some of us have come to equate manners with parental authority. We may confuse manners with restraint and inhibition, repressing a free spirit, but manners instruction really is a kind of behavioral training in consideration—in generosity of spirit—what is more freeing than generosity?

> Etiquette comes to us from the French. Originally it meant a soldier's billet for lodgings, then an identification label or ticket. Still later, the word came to designate the complex body of cere-monial rules governing the royal court of France. Finally it entered the English language about 1750 with its present meaning: the cus-tomary rules of conduct in a civilized society.[3]

We should make an impeccable impression not just at the table, but on the phone, on sales calls, and even online. The one who does will sail with ease up the corporate ladder.

As a teacher, trainer, speaker, and consultant in business and social etiquette for sixteen years, I wrote this book at the request of my stu-dents in the business and professional community.

My expertise comes from training, research, and experience. My interactive seminars—with participants from entry-level workers to board chairmen, chief executive officers, and members of the academic world—have shown me much of what is correct and accepted in today's business world.

Each chapter will begin with a short list of questions for the reader to test his or her EQ (Etiquette Quotient). The answers will be found in the same chapter.

CHAPTER 1

Rudeness Is Rampant

There is no accomplishment so easy to acquire
as politeness, and none more profitable.
George Bernard Shaw

An honest "Excuse me" is the grease that eases the
friction of human interaction. It's the bumper between
bodies on the verge of collision. It's a little peace
offering in the daily combat of urban life.
Mary Schmich

What Is Your EQ (Etiquette Quotient)? Business Etiquette

1. When was the last time you were the target of rude behavior?

2. Are you always confident about your choices in business protocol?

3. Why is there a heightened interest in business etiquette training today, and who brought it back?

4. What are the three Cs of business success?

Who Needs It?

It's Monday morning. You are finally out the door and on your way to work. As usual, the freeway looks crowded. Inconsiderate drivers make it almost impossible for you to merge with traffic from the highway entrance ramp. When you need to change lanes, no one will let you enter. Out of nowhere a car zooms up from behind and rides your bumper until you move over or get run down. You glance down and realize your son left the gas tank empty.

With frazzled nerves, you get to your office building. Your arms are full with demo equipment as you struggle to open the door that no one offers to open for you. What a way to start the day! If this is any indication of what's to come during the week, you wish you could go back and start over.

> 72 percent of Americans think the driving etiquette of others has gotten worse in the past 10 years.[1]

Where Did All the Manners Go?

Whatever happened to good, old-fashioned manners—consideration for the needs and feelings of others—like leaving some gasoline in the tank when you borrow the car or having a little courtesy on the highway? A silent communication with other drivers on the road should permit a simple courtesy of give and take. As we see drivers struggle with the same traffic needs we experience from time to time, we shouldn't need a manners patrol officer to arbitrate our acts of rude behavior on the roadway, but often we do.

In Charlotte, North Carolina, the police chief uses reported license plates to identify offending motorists and mail them shame-on-you notes. Last year, he sent 340 notices similar to this one: "Your vehicle was observed slowing unnecessarily and then speeding up to prevent being passed." [2]

Starting with the hippies in the '60s, and deteriorating in the '70s and '80s, standards of propriety in our society have plunged to extreme rudeness. It sometimes seems no one cares about good manners. Young people with advanced degrees and technical skills are seen chewing gum, chowing down, walking out of restaurants with toothpicks hanging from their mouths, letting doors fly back in someone's face, and showing up for work in what appears to be their weekend grubs. What is responsible for this rampant rudeness? Sadly, many of these young, highly trained professionals don't even realize they are being rude.

Our busy, rushed schedules are partly to blame. Often both parents work, leaving little time for dinner conversation about values and the Golden Rule—or even dinner together at all. Parents find it difficult to teach their children good dining habits and other rules of polite behavior. Running from one event to another, we have become victims of our schedules, appointments, and Daytimers.

> The problem of incivility cuts across all class and racial lines. "In the recent survey of educators by the American Association of School Administrators, the teaching of the golden rule—treat others as you want to be treated—was found to be an urgent necessity."[3]

Why Do We Need Rules Anyway?

The National Highway Traffic Safety Board recently reported to a congressional committee that a third of the car crashes and two-thirds of the resulting fatalities are caused by aggressive drivers.[4]

Aggressive drivers speed, tailgate, fail to yield, weave in and out of traffic, pass on the right, make improper lane changes, run stop signs, make hand and facial gestures, scream, honk, and flash their lights. They even commit murder. According to a recent news report, a man on a bicycle shot and killed a driver who bumped his bike.

Just as we need traffic rules to avoid chaos—not to mention danger—on the highways, we also need a common language of social skills. We like to meet, talk, dine, and do business efficiently in a pleasant atmosphere without embarrassing ourselves or someone else. We need to feel understood and cared about.

Years ago, we were a rural people living on farms that were miles apart. A farmer might not interact with other people for hours or days. Today, however, we live in crowded communities and work in partitioned work spaces where privacy is not an option. In today's technological jungle we find ourselves working and living elbow to elbow. Without a code of proper conduct, we become almost uncivilized.

Traffic regulations are the etiquette rules of driving a vehicle. Proper behavior is the etiquette of dealing civilly with others in our urban society.

Who Started the Return to Good Manners in Business?

The clarion call to return to proper etiquette did not come from some ladies' afternoon tea party; it came from the business community. New employees were leaving bad impressions on clients and customers, driving away business.

Still no one wanted to tell these young people their manners were offensive. The subject of etiquette has often been treated like the subject of sex used to be: No one talks about it. Few people will tell us when we make a blunder. Then if they do, we almost die of embarrassment.

Therefore, etiquette trainers and consultants have now been called in to the business environment to do the correcting on every topic imaginable, from poor grooming to sexual harassment. Their goal is to provide information and answer questions without embarrassing the individuals.

COMMON COURTESIES

- Saying "Please," "Thank you," "Excuse me," "Pardon me," and "May I"
- Asking someone to be seated
- Showing a visitor or guest to the door
- Holding the door for someone behind you
- Writing thank-you notes promptly

NEGATIVE GESTURES

- Walking in front of someone
- Cracking knuckles
- Backslapping
- Using toothpicks in public
- Chewing gum in public
- Coughing/sneezing uncovered
- Checking your watch
- Interrupting
- Pointing
- Staring
- Whispering
- Fidgeting
- Laughing loudly

The Three Cs of Success

Successful people possess three common characteristics: they are competent in their skills, confident in demeanor, and considerate of others. Etiquette directly affects the last two characteristics—confidence and consideration. When we know the behavior others expect of us, we turn self-consciousness into self-confidence, thereby allowing us to show consideration for others. We create an atmosphere that frees us to then focus on being competent in our jobs. This is especially important as companies streamline and downsize their labor force to reduce costs. Becoming successful is now more competitive than ever.

It is not illegal to be obnoxious and rude. No manners police will put us in jail, however, we will probably experience the pain of disapproval, the loss of a valued client, or a failed business deal because of a mistake in etiquette. Knowing the proper behavior that business associates expect makes it easier to take care of business successfully. We must know the rules of proper business protocol to escape embarrassing ourselves, our hosts, or our guests.

A Tidal Wave of Rudeness

Ripples of rudeness have become tidal waves of improper conduct. Although we are not left completely at the mercy of the rude, it is difficult to tell an employee that his or her impolite behavior ruined a business deal.

The issue of etiquette is very personal and often uncomfortable to address. It is easier to tell employees to improve their computer skills than to insist that they say hello to coworkers every morning. Yet without the pleasantries, teams become dysfunctional, relationships can become strained, and general morale is lowered. Civility is simply treating others with respect—courtesy. When it's absent, relationships deteriorate and productivity decreases.

This book is not about how to serve high tea to a British ambassador. It is about practical, solid business etiquette—the code of the business community. As a ready reference for everyday dilemmas dealing with business manners, it will detail the acceptable ways of behaving and responding that no one else will tell us (except perhaps our mother), and the faux pas that kill careers, relationships, and chances of promotion. The first area we will examine is the changing roles of men and women in the business world.

CHAPTER 2

The Changing Roles of
Men and Women

One of the top five trends today
is a "redefinition of gender roles."
Van Wisbard, The American Future

What Is Your EQ? New Roles for Men and Women in Business

1. How do business etiquette rules differ from social rules?
2. When does a breach of business etiquette become sexual harassment?
3. Who enters a revolving door first?
4. What are the rules when the boss is a woman?
5. What are the rules when women travel alone or with male colleagues?

New Roles for Men and Women

Life was simpler when all we had to do was "mind our manners" and practice the Golden Rule. That was before we advanced into the high-tech years, before *Megatrends 2000* alerted us to the coming global economy.[1] Now the business world has exploded into international markets.

Perhaps nothing in the business world has changed more in the last twenty-five years than the roles of men and women. The difference is measurable. According to the National Institute of Business Management, Inc., in 1991 only 2 percent of the Institute's literature was devoted to male/female protocol.[2] In 1995, 11 percent addressed the special concerns of male/female interaction in the marketplace.[3]

Participants in my classes and seminars have many questions concerning male/female protocol. They want to know when to apply the social rules and when to apply the business rules. Only dining questions come in as a close second.

Is chivalry dead? Yes and no. Chivalry (the way a gentleman behaves around ladies) is based on the old social rules. Traditionally, women in *social* circles are extended more courtesies than men. In business today, however, we try to be gender blind. Theoretically men and women are equal in all areas of employment, although realistically and practically they are still noticeably different in appearance, strength, and size.

Women have made great strides in their career achievements, but this has left many men confused. Some businesswomen want to be treated like "one of the guys." Others want equal opportunity advancement, but prefer to work with gentlemen who treat them as ladies. In a given situation a man may not be sure of a woman's preference, therefore, he must try to accommodate both types of working women.

Business/Social Interactions

Before the '70s, when men held most of the employment positions and women stayed home, the social rules about relationships were all we had to learn. When women entered the workplace in large numbers, questions began to arise. As a result, we now have business etiquette rules as well as social etiquette rules. The good news is that the business rules are less complicated because they are based on one criterion—rank. Social etiquette is based on age and gender. Business etiquette is based solely on rank or position—the pecking order.[4]

Problems do surface, however, when the business world intermingles with the social. We may find ourselves attending a business function away from our desk, where the atmosphere is more party-like. Food may also be part of the picture.

For example, there is the office Christmas party where spouses who are not coworkers may attend. Another time the lines blur is at a business meeting in a restaurant. Somehow we feel more relaxed and sociable when we dine. Should we use the social rules or the business rules of interaction? (When the rule is not clear, base your decision on common sense and observe the preferences of individuals as much as you can determine them.)

Many dilemmas face working people today when all that most of us want is simply to get on with business. Yet it is not always easy to "do business as usual." We need to know the business/social code for those times when the lines merge between business and social etiquette.

THE CODE

Proper etiquette in business is based on rank. After that it is simply looking out for the other person's comfort and never embarrassing anyone.

Before we deal with specifics, the new mentality required by the changes in the business community must be addressed. The businessperson's attitude and philosophy are key to smoothing over the rough places while doing business in our changing world.

Attitude

When relating to women, a man's attitude is critical. The key to making the right decision about behavior is to exhibit a non-condescending attitude or demeanor; otherwise, a man's good intentions can get him into a harassment suit.

In business, he must consider how his actions will be perceived. In other words, his behavior cannot be based solely on what he considers to be perfect gentlemanly behavior, but what is appropriate for the particular business circumstances.

A man should never call attention to his behavior as a gentleman. If he says, "Let me get that heavy door for you, honey," implying that the coworker is of the weaker sex, he is patronizing her. His attitude speaks louder than his actions.

"Gender distinctions have no relevance in the workplace today. Responsibilities should always be defined on the basis of job title and description, not on a gender basis."[5]

Although age and gender should not enter the decision, the man who finds himself in a business/social dilemma can often make a judgment based on the generation from which the woman comes. If she does not appear to be in a competitive situation with him, she may look more kindly on his efforts to be a gentleman. However, if she is vying with him for the top management position within the company, she may prefer to lead rather than follow.

Unspoken Understandings

In the business community of the '90s, there is often an "unspoken understanding" among employees, colleagues, and clients. Men who attend the same meetings, dine, or travel with women often recognize the women's preferences and comply with them. These men and women come to an unspoken understanding. The man offers to show deference to the woman, and she silently accepts or politely refuses.

For instance, if a man rises when a businesswoman enters a meeting, leaves, or returns to their table in a restaurant, she can ignore it or acknowledge the show of courtesy with a smile while saying, "Please keep your seat." Usually, she must say this only once during the course of the business day.

Opening Doors in the Workplace

Daily we encounter revolving doors, push doors, and pull doors. Opening doors for others is simply a physical recognition of the dignity of another person. It may seem unnecessary to discuss who should open a door, yet the topic comes up in every class I teach. Businessmen, especially in the South, often feel uncomfortable allowing a female to open a door for them. (Note: It is still acceptable in the South for the male to open doors unless he knows the woman prefers otherwise.) Letitia Baldrige, noted expert in business protocol, says to move quickly to open a door for anyone walking nearby who has his or her hands full.[6]

General business etiquette rules say that subordinate employees (whether male or female) should reach a door first and open it for senior executives. Taking turns in opening doors is often appropriate when walking with peers.

Revolving Doors

The junior employee, the host, or the stronger individual should enter a revolving door first to position it. He or she waits for the other person to enter the next compartment, then starts moving the door.

Push Doors

The subordinate employee should pass through a push door first and hold it open for the senior person. The employee should stand clear of the doorway, otherwise two people are uncomfortably touching each other as the second one tries to squeeze through the crowded doorway.

Restaurant Doors

Men often ask me what to do when they open a restaurant door and a crowd of people march through leaving one man in an awkward "holding" pattern. One solution is to move away from the door until he can barely reach it, hoping someone with the crowd of people will take his place. Another tactic is to make eye contact and hold the gaze of the first male adult he sees, as though he were turning the duty over to him.

Three general truths about doors:
- Junior ranking people should open and hold doors for senior ranking people.
- Doors should be opened and held for customers and clients.
- Assistance should be given to persons with a disability.

A restaurant often has an outer door with a small area between it and the door that opens into the main restaurant. Socially, a man opens the outer door for his spouse or companion, who waits in the anteroom for him to open the second door. If someone else opens the second door, the individual waits in the main lobby of the restaurant. Sometimes the female or "honored" individual opens the second door and waits inside, if circumstances warrant it.

In a survey, "seventy-seven percent [of the industries and companies responding] wrote that it is considered etiquette at their company for a man to open the door for a woman; 57 percent said it was etiquette for a woman to open the door for a man."[7]

Sexual Harassment

The words *sexual harassment* became part of our everyday vocabulary in the workplace when the Anita Hill versus Clarence Thomas hearings were televised. Sexual harassment is nothing new, but with the increasing number of women working outside the home, the number of complaints and charges has multiplied.[8]

COMPARISON OF THE ACCEPTABLE
PRACTICES IN THE 1970S TO THE 1990S

The following is an interesting comparison between a business etiquette book published in 1979 and those published today:

Executive Etiquette, by Marjabelle Young Stewart and Marian Faux, published in 1979 states: "Assuming that you want . . . to reject the pass, then try to find a gracious way to do so. After all, it is flattering to be liked by someone, and just because the someone happens to be a colleague is no reason to take offense."

"Try to temper a rejection with an honest compliment if at all possible. (You can, of course, decide to take a man up on his sexual overtures—a not uncommon occurrence these days in many offices.)"[9]

In the '90s we discuss "rejecting the pass" in court. That is how much our society has changed.

Dr. Louise Fitzgerald, a psychologist at the University of Illinois, says that some harassment is the result of a "cultural lag."[10] Many men entered the workplace at a time when sexual teasing and innuendo were commonplace. They must now be alerted that this behavior is no longer appropriate nor wise.

In 1964, the Civil Rights Act defined harassment and allowed workers to sue because of discrimination based on sex, race, or disability. In 1991, employees who brought such lawsuits were allowed a jury trial and awarded cash damages.

In 1980, the Equal Employment Opportunity Commission issued its guidelines and definition of sexual harassment. In 1986, the Supreme Court expanded the definition to include subtle forms of intimidation such as lingering, intimate touches, or repeated sexual comments about aspects of a person's physique. These actions were said to create a "hostile environment."

According to Phillips in *The Concise Guide to Executive Etiquette*, sexual harassment is defined as "unwelcome sexual advances . . . or other verbal or physical conduct of a sexual nature . . . where submission to such conduct is explicitly or implicitly . . . a condition of [the] individual's employment, . . . used as a basis for employment decisions, . . . interferes with work performance or creates an intimidating working environment."[11]

> "In business, people are supposed to treat each other equally and act according to rules of protocol (based on rank), not of gender, and one sex is supposed to come to the aid of the other whenever either needs assistance." *Letitia Baldrige, Protocol Officer of the White House*

In a 1988 survey, *Working Woman* magazine found that ignoring sexual harassment cost a typical *Fortune 500* company more than six million dollars a year in absenteeism, lost productivity, and employee turnover.[12] In the relatively short time from the '70s to the end of the '80s, complaints of sexual harassment jumped 70 percent.

More than 45 percent of New England management firms admitted in a survey that their companies had dealt with sexual harassment in and out of the courts in the past year. That number climbs daily.[13]

Breach of Etiquette or Harassment

When does a breach of etiquette become harassment? The National Institute of Business (91) says, "If you are pursued beyond two rejections or if threats, bribes or physical force are used against you," the next step should be to go "through a corporate complaint process."[14]

How to Avoid Disaster

Remember that the office is not the place to discuss your marital affairs, nor is it the place for romance. Scrutinize your behavior with the opposite sex so that seemingly innocent gestures like putting your hand on someone's shoulder or a quick hug are not misconstrued as romantic actions. A male who places his arm around a female executive or coworker's shoulder exercises poor judgment. Experts suggest both men and women avoid any touching of the opposite sex that might be misinterpreted as sexual harassment. Only light, brief touching in a neutral zone such as the elbow or shoulder is permitted. Touching superiors of either sex is always taboo, except to shake hands. Also avoid any conversation that might make someone turn red with embarrassment.

In the office, a woman appears more assertive and businesslike if she places her hands on the armrests of her chair and not in her lap. A woman should avoid seemingly innocent actions such as brushing back her hair or crossing and uncrossing her legs since such gestures "can be interpreted as provocative."

Career counselors suggest the following additional guidelines to avoid possible accusations of sexual harassment:

- Keep meetings in public and within typical office hours.
- If you must meet before or after typical work hours, take along your spouse or another colleague.
- Do not go home first and change to after-five clothes.
- Stick to the topics of business at hand.

- Call someone of the opposite sex, regardless of their marital status, within working hours and not in the evening or during the weekend.

Relating to the Boss

More and more women are becoming executives—even CEOs—in today's rapidly changing workforce. It can be quite confusing as men and women try to deal with new situations. Yet "etiquette is just what people need to guide their behavior in these unsettled times."[15]

> In social situations, it is still permissible for men to rise for women, help with their coats, pull out their chair, and pay the check.

When a Woman Works for a Female Boss

A problem can arise when two women do not hold equal status. The subordinate, or even the superior, may inappropriately cross the line of informality simply because she is relating to someone of the same sex. One woman may feel comfortable confiding in the other in a way she would never behave if the boss were a male. However, it is usually a mistake to deviate from the rules of business etiquette that say it is inappropriate to share intimate, personal details with those who are either superior or subordinate to you. That inappropriate confession may sabotage your advancement or later make you uncomfortable around the one in whom you confided.

To avoid such a situation, treat any executive according to the etiquette appropriate for anyone at that level, not according to the gender of the person. The issue is not how a woman should treat a woman or how a woman should treat a man. It is how to treat a businessperson in a work-related social or business situation.

When a Man Works for a Female Boss

The Complete Office Handbook, presents the following guidelines for men working for a female boss:

- Avoid offers of help that have sexual connotations, such as "Since you are a woman, you will need help from a man—feel free to call me."
- Let your female boss say whether your relationship will be formal or informal. For instance, she will decide the use of first names or a title and last name.
- Do not misinterpret her friendliness as a romantic overture.
- Allow your female boss to set the time and place for work-related duties.
- Treat her with the same respect you would grant a male executive.[16]

When a Female Works for a Male Boss

- A male boss should call a female employee by her first name only if she is told to address him in the same manner.
- Be willing to share some of the chores, such as getting the coffee for both of you when one of you is busy.

> If a woman walking beside a man down a corridor wants to open the door for herself, she will usually walk a step ahead and reach for it. If she is more traditional, she will step out of the way to allow the man to do the honors.

Finally, let the rules of business protocol always guide your conduct, regardless of the age or gender of the superior or subordinate. Specific rules for opening doors, rising, assisting with coats, and similar actions can be adjusted within each office or company. If you are new to the company, observe the actions of other subordinates with superiors. In all man/woman issues, find out what is expected at your company by observing or asking a trusted colleague.

Out-of-Town Meetings

Another awkward situation arises when business meetings are held at a hotel. The meetings should be scheduled in public or in reserved conference rooms if possible. The person who runs the meeting should consider how the other attendees might feel about the meeting's location. Many hotels offer a sitting room with no beds, or the hotel will reserve a meeting room in a separate section of the hotel, usually just off the lobby.

Traveling Together

Men and women traveling together should exhibit behavior toward each other that reflects their status within the organization, not their gender. In other words, other travelers and diners who see them together will quickly know they are discussing business. Traveling together should not be an excuse to switch from business to social manners.

The Businesswoman Traveling Alone

Sometimes a businesswoman must travel alone. Because this is becoming more common, fellow travellers usually understand that a woman travelling alone is not a signal that she is available. If she dresses and conducts herself professionally, she will be seen as a confident businesswoman. Here are some basic tips to make the trip safe and businesslike:

- When arriving at the hotel, identify yourself to the concierge and to the manager and tell why you are in the hotel. You may want to tip the concierge and the bellboy well. Always carry an adequate supply of one-dollar and five-dollar bills when you travel.
- A hotel room or suite is not the ideal place to hold a business meeting, but if there is no other choice, make sure no personal items are visible, except perhaps a framed picture of your family. If your bed must be used as a conference table, have chairs arranged around it. You may provide soft drinks and coffee.
- You may prefer to eat in the hotel restaurant, where you can control the environment. Your entrance into the hotel lounge or restaurant reveals whether you are comfortable in your surroundings.
- When dining alone, make a reservation beforehand. Usually, the better the restaurant, the better you will be treated. If you are not satisfied with your table, request a better one if it is available.

Rule of Thumb

In summary, it is important to remember that in the workplace men and women alike should base their conduct on corporate rank. The rules for business etiquette emanate from a respect for the person's position, not from gender differences or character traits.

CHAPTER 3

First Impressions and Body Language

The goal is to turn self-consciousness
into self-confidence.
Bess McFadden Sanders, Founder
The Graces/Gentle-Man Company

What Is Your EQ? Projecting a Professional Image

1. What are the six *S*s of making a professional impression?
2. Why should our speech be free of word pollution?
3. What does your body language say about you?
4. What is the correct distance to stand from someone?
5. When do others judge our footwear and what does it tell them?

The Importance of a First Impression

In golf when we bungle the first tee shot, we get a free one called a mulligan. Unfortunately, there is never a second chance to make a first impression. People usually form their opinion of us in the first thirty seconds of seeing us by judging our appearance, our visual communication, and our speech. They evaluate our inner qualities later.

> It takes 15 seconds to make a first impression, but it may take the rest of your life to change a bad one.

Although dressing to conform may not always be our preference, it is the best approach in business. Whether we like it or not, the standard is set by those in authority and is dictated by our work environment. We gain credibility and confidence by the way we present ourselves.

For instance, men who work in financial institutions usually wear laced, wing-tipped or capped-toed shoes. Laced, plain-toed shoes are also appropriate. Women wear mid-heel, closed pumps.

For people who handle other people's money, dressing conservatively is the most appropriate dress. Yet in the landscaping business, top management may wear jeans and boots on the job, but they must be of high quality.

A good rule of thumb is to dress, if possible, for the position we would like to have. Our current salary may mean that each day we choose from only two well-tailored suits instead of the many suits our superiors own, but quality is more important than quantity.

Making a Positive First Impression

Packaging ourselves with (a) the right code of behavior, (b) the proper attire, (c) appropriate speech, and (d) good body language may determine whether we get the job we want. The wrong packaging of ourselves may not mean the loss of our jobs, but it can reduce our job security in today's climate of downsizing. Companies are reducing the number of people in their labor force to cut costs.

Proper Code of Behavior

The business code is a set of etiquette rules. We seldom enjoy playing a game without first learning the rules. We may learn some of the game by observation, but to succeed we must read or hear the fine points of the game. Nothing builds confidence like knowing the rules of the game.

Meeting and greeting in business involves the six Ss: (1) stand, (2) smile, (3) see, (4) shake, (5) speak, and (6) say. Learning and using the six Ss allows us to focus on other people. It also portrays confidence. If we don't utilize the six Ss we tend to think only about what we are going to say and do next. We often don't remember the name of the person we are meeting, and we appear to be ill at ease.

Making a good impression requires that we show more interest in the other person than ourselves. We all know people who remember names and always seem relaxed and affable. We like and remember those people.

The six Ss are:

(1) Standing—for senior personnel and when greeting or meeting others shows respect and deference.

(2) A Smile—by one person usually encourages one from another. It takes only twelve muscles to smile, but it takes seventy-two to frown.

(3) Seeing—into a person's eyes means we are friendly, that we are interested in the other person.

> In the Middle Ages a knight wearing armor with a metal shield over his head lifted the eye covering to expose his eyes, showing that he was a friend. That is the tradition behind a man tipping his hat (touching the brim when he sees a lady).

(4) Shaking—hands is the proper greeting for Americans when dealing with fellow Americans. Our handshake should be firm (not crushing) and dry. The web between our thumb and index finger should meet the web of the other person's hand. If necessary, we should wipe our hand before extending it.

(5) Speaking—our name slowly and distinctly is important.

(6) Saying—the new acquaintance's name back to him or her when we are introduced helps us remember it, and people like to hear their name used in a friendly manner.

Proper Business Attire and Grooming

Our clothing, accessories, and grooming are the first things people notice. New acquaintances judge our confidence and our competence by our appearance. Does wearing expensive, trendy clothing and accessories automatically say that we are dressed appropriately? Not necessarily.

Clothing. Faddish clothes that send the wrong message are often crumpled, poorly fitted, or do not reflect the proper image for the business. They suggest a slovenly, unkempt individual who will do sloppy work.

Noisy or gaudy accessories also spoil a professional image. Paying attention to the details of our appearance implies that we can be trusted with the details demanded by the job.

One might argue that ability should be all that matters, but "Job applicants who project the professional image effectively . . . command higher starting salaries—as much as 20 percent—than those who do not."[1]

If we are not sure how to choose quality, we should shop at a retail store that offers professional advice in business apparel. Clothing in those stores usually costs a little more, but it will be of better quality and last longer than cheaper garments. We should also check our footwear. Unpolished shoes with run-down heels indicate we don't pay attention to detail.

Grooming. Personal grooming should be impeccable at all times, especially the twelve inches above our shoulders, because people look there first. Have you ever talked to someone after lunch who had a piece of lettuce wedged in their front teeth?

We should privately check our appearance in a mirror on a regular basis. Proper grooming includes overall cleanliness; neat, clean-smelling hair; light, daytime makeup or a well-shaven face; clean, well-trimmed nails; and fresh dental hygiene. If cologne or perfume is used it should whisper, not shout.

Appropriate Speech

The words we choose brand us as either professional or amateurish. People listen for good grammar and properly chosen (although not necessarily big) words. Repetitive phrases, profanity, slurs, foul language, and derogatory nicknames for people of other cultures distract from a professional, businesslike image. Our words should be positive. We should sound good as well as look good.

Many words and phrases today have a "short shelf life." Savvy businesspeople watch closely for signs of yesterday's good phrase becoming a tired cliche today. They adjust their speech to fit the time and the vernacular of the individual to whom they are speaking.

Also beware of creating a "Tower of Babel" with double-talk. Don't assume the person you are talking to understands your slang, jargon, cliches, euphemisms, acronyms, idioms, slogans, colloquialisms, and oxymorons. Avoid or completely remove the following types of speech from your professional conversation.

Repetitive Phrases. One trap many of us fall into is using "filler" words. One example in conversation is filling silences with "um" or "uh" or ending sentences with meaningless phrases such as "ya' know?" and "okay?" Our listeners often hear nothing we say except the "all right?" after every sentence.

Slang. Slang expressions can cause miscommunication or even no communication if the expression is understood only in a particular region or industry. Such words include *classy* for elegant and *dough* or *bread* for money. Sometimes young business people lapse into slang speech mistakenly trying to show they are "one of the regular guys" (a euphemistic phrase).

Cliches. An overused, trite expression is a cliche. Some examples include: The buck stops here; shotgun approach; run of the mill; down the tubes; seat-of-the-pants operation; dog-and-pony-show; interface the system.

> Recently I spoke to a group called Friendship International. Many were new to this country. Choosing my words carefully, I tried to speak without jargon or euphemisms. Afterwards a woman approached me and asked, "What does 'bottom line' mean?" As you can see, even etiquette teachers have difficulty sometimes.

Euphemisms. Mild, indirect expressions such as "See ya' round" are euphemisms. In business, poor communication can be costly. We must make sure our information is clear and businesslike. Instead of "see ya' round," a professional might say, "I will call you tomorrow with a definite dollar amount for that project."

> In the 1988 Olympics in South Korea, NBC designed a T-shirt with the slang expression "We're Bad." The shirts were an attempt to encourage our U.S. boxers; however the slogan was taken literally. It created an international incident.[2]

Jargon. Lingo or jargon is a specialized vocabulary that workers in the same occupation use to communicate among themselves. It is somewhat like shorthand speech. While jargon can save time and be useful to coworkers, using it with "outsiders" is rude. We cannot expect those outside the company or organization to communicate with us when we use terms that are incomprehensible to them.

A word or term familiar throughout an industry may be vague to others. For example, during the break in a recent class for the U.S.A. Rice Federation, the participants were discussing "blast." When I looked puzzled, they explained that it is a disease they fear will infest their rice crops. I would never have guessed that.

Acronyms. Words formed from the first letters of several words make up an acronym. Some are familiar to most of us: UPS for United Parcel Service, CEO for chief executive officer, U.S.A. for United States of America, and NEA for National Endowment for the Arts, which can also stand for National Education Association.

Terms specific to one business or industry can be "Greek" to another. To a computer technician *GIGO* means "garbage in, garbage out." To those unfamiliar with the world of computers GIGO means nothing. Another example is the term *RAM/ROM* used for temporary versus permanent memory on computers.

Titles and job descriptions can also be confusing to the general public. One company's account executive is another company's salesperson. One organization's secretary is another group's administrative assistant.

All personnel should be careful when communicating with others. It's important to anticipate the need of the person with whom we are dealing. We must differentiate between our own technical knowledge and the average person's general information. It is uncomfortable for those outside the organization to say, "I don't know what you are talking about."

Oxymorons. A pair of English words that contradict each other is an oxymoron. Examples of oxymorons include jumbo shrimp, metal wood (in golf), and guest host.

According to Roger Axtell in *Do's and Taboos Around the World*, American business people are especially guilty of language misuse. He adds these to the list: hacker, computer virus, leveraged buyouts, power lunch, and number crunching.[3]

Word Pollution. We are engulfed with "word pollution"—the use of offensive words—in our culture today. Sometimes it seems we will drown in profanity and derogatory nicknames that demean people who are "different" from us. We should completely rid our speech of these words.

According to the *World Book Encyclopedia Dictionary*, the word *profane* is defined as an adjective showing "contempt or disregard for God or holy things."[4] To use profanity is "to blaspheme." "*Swear* is another term for profanity. It suggests using holy names to express strong feelings."[5]

Derogatory nicknames insult people of other ethnic or socioeconomic groups just as profanity insults God and those who believe in Christ. Any savvy businessperson is careful not to assume that everyone is of the same background. Besides being offensive, such terms can be hazardous to personal success.

Foul language. This type of inappropriate language includes words that characterize bodily functions.

> "Recently graduated MBAs seem to think it's perfectly all right to [use foul language and profanity]. It's not all right. It tarnishes the image of the company."[6]

Visual Communication

> A judge in New Orleans declared a mistrial and ruled that the plaintiff's attorney "prejudiced the jury through eye contact and body language."[7]

Body language plays an important role in our professional image. Our nonverbal communication accounts for at least 55 percent of the perception others have of us. People get nonverbal signals from our mannerisms. Often our gestures are unconscious, but they can enhance or destroy our visual image.

Our habitual gestures, stance, use of eye contact, and overall demeanor tell people if we are nervous, relaxed, confident, shy, tired, lazy, indifferent, etc.

David McNeill, a professor of psychology and linguistics at the University of Chicago, has devoted almost thirty years to studying body language. He says at least half of language is imagery and that gestures play out that image more spontaneously than words. Therefore the spontaneous movements of our bodies reveal what we are really thinking. [8]

He goes on to say, "Gesture is a hand movement that is as much a part of language as speech." So not all body language is bad. He encourages us by saying, "The more articulate and well-educated a person is, the more likely you are to see gesture." [9]

"As much as 95 percent of communication is nonverbal. Body language is the oldest and most trusted language in the world," says Marilyn Maple, a professor of education at the University of Florida. [10]

Psychiatrist Robert Hales also says that we should believe what we see. Words can be manipulated, but gestures are a lot harder to control. [11]

Nonetheless, in conducting business we must make sure we use only appropriate gestures that are in good taste. Ask a trusted friend to tell you privately if you have any annoying habits. Even family members may sometimes give unsolicited advice about our idiosyncrasies which we should hear and evaluate.

Consider the job interview of two highly qualified applicants. One gave a limp handshake with her fingers only and looked at the floor as she talked. The other had a grip that could break bone, and he tried to stare down the interviewer. The visual image of the first one said she was timid. The body language of the other one said that he was overly confident, maybe even arrogant. Neither applicant was hired for the job.

> "Your manners are always under examination by committees little suspected . . . awarding or denying you very high prizes when you least think of it." *Ralph Waldo Emerson*

Eye contact is also important. It is "the most remembered element in forming an impression," says Nancy Austin, management consultant and author. [12] Try to avoid staring—five to seven seconds is the maximum amount of time for a meeting of the eyes before looking at another feature of the face.

Here are some additional nonverbal don'ts we can turn into do's.

- *Don't* take the "fig leaf stance." Speakers who clasp their hands in front with straight arms forming a long *V* appear insecure.
- *Do* keep your arms loosely at your sides in a fluid position.
- *Don't* be a "terminator" with a brutal handshake, but avoid extending a lifeless palm dangling from a limp wrist.
- *Do* hold your fingers and thumb as if you were holding a gun. Extend them directly, clasp well for a few seconds with the *V* of your hand meeting the *V* of the other person's hand, then release the handshake.

- *Don't* be a "space invader" by standing within someone's personal space around them.
- **Do** show respect for invisible personal boundaries—about eighteen inches.
- *Don't* put up a "roadblock" by folding your arms across your chest. Such posture indicates strong resistance.
- **Do** leave the arms open. Lean forward to show attentiveness.
- *Don't* be a "pickpocket." When you put your hand in your pocket, those standing nearby wonder what you are hiding.
- **Do** keep your hands in sight.
- *Don't* be a "back patter." It is patronizing. We pat children.
- **Do** keep a hands-off posture. In business relationships, do not touch—except to shake hands.
- *Don't* be a "comfort fidgeter." Rocking back and forth and tugging on your ear may satisfy some personal comfort need, but such habits actually increase stress.
- **Do** try to be relaxed.
- *Don't* stand ramrod stiff trying to avoid all these don'ts. Simply make sure you do nothing in excess.

(More on gestures in chapter 12.)

Because our body speaks for us, we should keep in mind what we are saying with the various parts.

Hands. Our hands should enhance what we say, not detract. Survey results show that when we keep our hands above the waist, we project a more positive image.

Arms. Crossing our arms across our chests with our hands tucked inside makes us appear defensive or indifferent.

Shoulders. "Hold your shoulders back" is a familiar admonition, but an unnatural position. We do better to maintain good posture. Pretend you have a string attached to your breastbone. By pulling the string from above, you lift your torso to a confident-looking position without drooping your shoulders or standing at "military attention."

Chin. Looking confident (not arrogant) is not that hard to do. With the chin level with the floor, be careful not to drop the eyes. Gazing downward makes us appear introverted or very shy. Keeping the chin too high indicates arrogance.

Eyes. When we look someone in the eye, we are focused and listening, alert and unafraid of reprisal. To make eye contact, we must feel good about ourselves. People unable to make eye contact may appear to be deceitful, as though they were hiding something. Eye contact simply means looking at a person's face during conversation. Some people practice in front of a mirror to overcome their inhibitions about eye contact.

Staring, on the other hand, is gazing into someone's eyes without ever looking at another feature of the face. Staring can give us that "being-off-in-some-other-place" appearance. To avoid staring we should look from a person's eyes to his or her mouth and back to the eyes.

Feet. What we do with our feet says a lot about our demeanor. When sitting erect with both feet on the floor, we are usually sitting near the front of the chair with our back straight. We appear to be alert, interested, and responsive.

Feet and Legs. Women should never cross their legs when on stage. Instead, turn both legs to one side and cross the ankles. Off stage, if we must cross one leg over the other, we should do so after we turn to one side or the other.

Bouncing the foot that is crossed or swinging a shoe from the toe is taboo.

Knees. A woman keeps her knees together when sitting—whether she is wearing pants or a skirt.

Walking. When walking, we should not shuffle, but walk briskly as though we have a destination.

Sitting. The way we sit in a chair reveals our attitude. Slouching or sprawling in a chair means we are indifferent or too relaxed for business. We exhibit a "don't care" attitude. The best seated position shows us with our feet on the floor with our back erect (not stiff.) We should sit on the front of the chair, if necessary, to keep our feet on the floor.

Proximity. Giving people "space" means standing eighteen to twenty-four inches from them—at least a forearm's length away. In conversation, if people often back away from you, they may feel that you are getting too close.

Fidgeting. Jingling change, twisting a strand of hair, jangling bracelets, shifting from side to side, and poking our hands down in our pockets all show nervousness.

> "... bedew no man's face with your spittle by approaching too near him when you speak."
> *George Washington's Rules of Civility & Decent Behavior*

The following are a few more habits that create a bad impression:
- Clearing your throat or running your tongue over your teeth
- Glancing at the floor
- Tossing, hitting, or throwing an imaginary ball
- Scratching
- Chewing your nails or chewing gum in public
- Drawing a necklace up into your mouth or rubbing it on your chin
- Picking at your cuticles or biting your nails
- Picking your teeth

In an increasingly competitive world, the businessperson who makes an impeccable impression will be the one who makes the deal or gets the big promotion.

CHAPTER 4

Telecommunications Etiquette

*When a client or customer speaks to a representative
of the company who has a gruff or uninterested
response and does not present a positive image,
the caller is likely to contact the competition.*
Marilyn Pincus and Arlene Connolly,
National Institute of Business Management, 1991

What Is Your EQ? Telecommunications

1. Is your business telephone answered before the third ring?
2. Can callers clearly understand the name of the company or organization when it is announced?
3. Are callers given the opportunity to decline being put on hold?
4. Are calls transferred successfully or transferred and lost?
5. What are the rules for cellular phones, beepers, conference calls, answering machines, and other telephone technology?

From the "new-hire" to the CEO, from the switchboard operator to the chairman of the board, telephone manners make a difference in the way the public perceives an organization. Telephone annoyances can destroy good business relationships, lose business, and reflect badly on all the employees.

> Speak unto others as you would have others speak unto you.

Eighty percent of today's business is conducted over the telephone. Its use is second only to the face-to-face meeting in terms of importance. The telephone presents certain challenges to communication because it prevents the nonverbal cues we use to judge our interactions with others in person. The way people dress, their eye contact, and the way they roll or shift their eyes when they make a statement is not visible for us to scrutinize over the telephone. Therefore we must listen carefully to know if the person is enthusiastic or agreeable. To get a picture of the other person we must rely on the timing of a pause, the length of a silence, noise in the background, or the quality of the voice.

Answering a Business Telephone

A telephone call is often the first contact an individual has with a company or organization. It is vital that each call be managed pleasantly and efficiently.

The Telephone Attendant

The person who answers the telephone may be the most important member of the office team. Whether he or she is part of a major corporation, a small business, a church staff, or a charity fund-raising organization, that voice represents every employee. It either enhances or damages the reputation of the business.

The one who answers the phones often gives the first and only impression of the company. Because first impressions are so important and enduring, a polite, knowledgeable employee should always answer a business phone. Telephone attendants must know how to locate personnel by name and extension number and be able to successfully direct calls.

Most callers need specific information or need to speak to a person who can give it to them, however, some callers are vague about who it is they want to reach and unclear about what they need. It is then the telephone attendant's task to ask polite questions, always leaving callers feeling that they were well served.

The telephone attendant should:

- know something about each employee's job description as well as the inner workings of the company in order to expedite calls politely and efficiently;

- give callers the extension number and the name of the person they are being transferred to in case the call gets disconnected;
- notify other employees before transferring calls to them; and
- ascertain that each call has been transferred successfully. Many offices have a "ring back" to the telephone attendant for transferred calls that go unanswered.

Telephone Manners That Make a Good Business Impression

- Never smoke, eat, or drink while talking on the telephone.
- Answer in as few rings as possible.
- Eliminate slang, jargon, and company lingo.
- Speak slowly and clearly. The caller cannot read your lips.
- Remember the priority of other incoming calls.
- Use the caller's name often. Always have pad and pencil ready.
- Never tell the other person to call back. Say, "I'll call you back" or "May I call you . . . ?"
- Avoid side conversations while you have a caller on the line.
- When reaching a wrong number, say "I am sorry" or "Sorry, I have the wrong number."
- Redial the call if you originated it and lose the connection.

How to Answer a Business Telephone

When answering the company telephone, an attendant should:
- answer with the company name, stating it cheerfully and clearly, "This is the XYZ Company. Good morning/afternoon. How may I direct your call?" or a similar request for information;

- answer with a vibrant voice;
- speak clearly and slowly; and
- show genuine interest in the caller and enthusiastically try to accommodate his or her needs.

A cold, expressionless voice does more damage over the telephone than in person. Face to face, we find it easier to show interest and liveliness than we do with our voices alone. Our voice and choice of words are our only means of communicating on the telephone. Therefore we must never let our voices reveal that the last caller was rude and insulting, or displace our anger onto the next caller. Every caller deserves to be treated as though he or she were the most important caller of the day.

If we answer abruptly, we sound rude or unfriendly. Being careful not to mumble, we must speak slowly and distinctly, especially when giving the company's name. The caller may not be sufficiently familiar with the company to unscramble a speedy rendition of the name. (It is easy to get lazy or impatient after saying the same name thirty or more times daily.)

In addition, the caller who hears a garbled name may not know if he or she has reached the intended number. I have often placed a call only to hear a voice on the other end rifle through the name so quickly that I was left confused. One time when I asked if I had reached a certain company, I received an irritated "That's what I just said!" At still other times, I have been unsure what the answerer said as I was quickly put on hold. Vowing never to call again, some customers hang up and take their business elsewhere.

We must listen attentively, not interrupting the caller except to make some remarks or sounds such as "um" from time to time to show agreement or disagreement. Such responses let the other person know we are still on the line and interested.

Who Is Responsible?

If you are the owner of the business or the supervisor, you must see to it that all telephone attendants are properly trained. The following three techniques are proven to improve their skills.

1. Supply the telephone attendants with mirrors. This allows them to watch their facial expressions as they talk on the phone. A smile can actually be heard because the tone and the lilt of the voice becomes more alert and enthusiastic.

2. Record the way incoming calls are handled. This allows us to:
   - listen for enthusiasm and a lively rhythm in the voice. If the caller hears a dull monotone, the answerer should get up and walk around occasionally to rejuvenate the brain. Moving around also helps us project energy through our telephone voice;
   - listen for courteous phrases such as "Thank you, Mr. Doolittle" or "It is good of you to call, Ms. Thistlewait," or whatever is appropriate; and
   - listen for the deliberate and frequent use of the caller's name.

3. Call one's own office periodically to check the manners of the one who answers the telephone.

Answering Your Own Telephone

Today, many high-level executives as well as subordinates answer their own phones. By doing so, they present an image that suggests accessibility, friendliness, and willingness to accommodate the caller.

In business, always identify yourself by first and last name when answering your own phone. If an assistant answers your phone first and tells you who is on the line, greet the caller by name, "Hello, Darlene. This is Russ Michaels."

If the caller asks if you are Russ Michaels before you have a chance to identify yourself, say, "This is he" or "This is Russ." Avoid saying, "Speaking"—it's too abrupt.

Screening Calls

Sometimes it is necessary to screen calls. When doing so our choice of methods and our comments are extremely important. We may find ourselves giving a customer or client a first impression of the entire organization. This may be the only opportunity to meet that customer, perhaps the only opportunity to sell our product or service and keep his or her business.

In a few businesses that are not customer dependent, the telephone attendant is told to say, "May I tell him (her) who is calling?" If the caller says no, the answerer may say, "He (she) likes to have your file in front of him (her) when talking to you." (Adapt the appropriate wording for your company or business.) For example, when a patient calls a doctor's office, the doctor or nurse can better answer the patient's concerns if he or she has the chart when returning the patient's call.

When the Boss Is Unavailable

Without some explanation, it is very insulting to hear that Mr. Executive "is not taking calls at this time." If the executive is unavailable, the person answering the phone may say something like, "Mr. Westcott is meeting with the human resources director. May I have your name and company? I will be happy to give him a message, or I can connect you with Ms. Kablewait who may be able to help you."

If the attendant routinely says, "He (or she) will call you back," then the boss is required to do so. Simply informing the boss of a call leaves the decision about returning it up to him or her.

When the boss does not want to accept a call, the attendant must make it clear at the outset. Otherwise the caller knows he is getting the runaround, and a runaround is a rude maneuver. For example, here is one approach—"Mr. Brown advises all suppliers to contact specific department heads. I can direct your call to the right person if you can give me more information."

If the boss is out, the attendant must inform the caller of that fact before asking the caller to give his or her name. The following example illustrates:

Telephone attendant: "The XYZ Company. Ms. Applewait's office. May I help you?"

Caller: "I want to speak to Ms. Applewait."

Attendant: "I am sorry, but Ms. Applewait is not in the office today (or at this time). She will return tomorrow. Please give me your name and company and I will give her your message. "

Placing a Caller on Hold

Nothing makes a client or customer angrier than to be put on hold and ignored. The telephone attendant should ask, "May I put you on hold?" and wait for a response. That gives the caller the option to call back. Perhaps the caller is on a wireless phone in his car where time is costly. The caller (who has already identified himself) can say, "Please tell Mr. Michaels that I called and that I will call back in a few minutes."

If the caller decides to wait "on hold," the operator keeps the caller informed regularly by saying, "I am sorry. Mr. Michaels is still on another line. Would you like to continue holding, or would you like to leave a message?" Callers should be kept on hold for no longer than twenty seconds without hearing a human voice to inform them of the status of their call. With several incoming calls, the operator must remember (or make note of) the priority of each call.

"Holding" situations happen to all of us. We always appreciate the courtesy of not being forgotten while we wait. This simple act of consideration shows that the company cares, and it makes a difference in the way outsiders perceive the entire organization.

Speaking Effectively on the Telephone

The following guidelines apply to all telephone users.

- If you think you may have reached a wrong number, ask if you have reached the number as you repeat it. If the answer is no, explain with, "I'm sorry. Please excuse the ring" or "Sorry, I must have dialed the wrong number." Saying nothing is extremely rude and unpleasant to the person who answers the phone.

- The mouthpiece should be about one inch from the speaker's mouth.

- If either party has an accent or speech impediment, the speaker should be patient and accommodate the other's limitation.

- All telephone users should refrain from chewing, drinking, sipping, slurping, rattling ice, opening mail, or sucking on candy. All these annoyances make rude sounds that magnify.

- Do not sneeze or cough during a telephone conversation if possible. If it is unavoidable, cover the mouthpiece of the phone so the sound is not heard. If you think the person on the other end of the line heard the noise, say, "Pardon me."

- When a telephone connection is broken, the caller re-places the call. In business it is prudent for the seller or service provider to call the customer back no matter who initiated the call.
- When using call-waiting, the one who temporarily leaves a call to answer a call-waiting signal should re-place the call if the first caller is lost—regardless who initiated the call.
- Never leave the first caller for more than ten seconds when you answer your call-waiting signal.
- The caller usually says goodbye first, but a businessperson allows a customer or client to end the conversation. To indicate closure, make sure all the customer's questions and needs are addressed. (For additional suggestions of how to end a conversation, see page 55).

Placing Your Own Calls

Many executives make their own telephone calls. Sometimes when an assistant makes the call it gives the impression that the executive is more important than the person receiving the call. This is especially true in the case of cancelling an appointment. If you cannot cancel personally, have another executive do it with apologies. A call from one's assistant can give the impression that the call is routine and the recipient is unimportant.

If an executive finds it necessary to have an assistant place a call to avoid wasting time going through several channels before reaching the right person, he must keep in mind that it is rude to initiate a call and then make the party wait. The executive should be available immediately.

When placing a call personally, always identify yourself (using your first and last name) and the name of your company or organization. For example, "Hello, this is Darlene Cooper of the XYZ Company. May I speak to Russ Michaels?" It is unfair (not to mention a waste of time) to expect people to guess or have to work at recognizing our voices even if they have talked to us often on the telephone.

As callers we should not be offended when asked to identify ourselves. Of course, if we say our name as soon as someone answers the phone, we don't have to worry about being quizzed.

It is rude to pretend to be on a first name basis with the boss in order to get past a receptionist. We should not assume first names. If in doubt, we should use the person's title and last name. The individual then has the option to say, "Please call me Joe."

When placing a call, we should remember that the person who screens it often has a great deal of influence over our message getting delivered. We must be friendly and polite to everyone. The tone we use makes a discernable difference. Our tone should show respect for the person who answers the phone regardless of our frustration or impatience.

Any unexpected call is an interruption. Therefore, it is a simple courtesy for us to ask if it is a convenient time to talk for the individual we call. He or she may prefer to set up a later time. If so, we should try to establish a specific time.

We should not be offended if someone asks us to call back later or asks to return our call. The individual may be in the middle of something that cannot be postponed. We must consider the way we would feel if the situation were reversed.

If the executive you want to reach is not available, be sure the person you are talking to understands your name. Give the reason for your call and your telephone number. Ask about a good time to call back.

If you are calling someone in a specific position, but you do not know that person's name, ask the operator or the person answering the phone to give it you. For example: Hello, I'm Alfred Knowles and I am with the XYZ Corporation. I would like to talk with your sales manager. Could you please give me the name and number and then ring it for me? Thank you."

Using Options in Telecommunications

Caller Identification (Caller ID)

Perhaps someone calls your telephone answering device without leaving a message. You recognize the number when you check Caller Identification on your phone. If you return the call, avoid saying his or her name until it is volunteered. The caller may be unfamiliar with Caller ID. It is disconcerting to have someone return your call when you did not leave a message.

Call-Waiting

With call-waiting you can ignore the beep and say, "I have call-waiting, but I'm not going to interrupt our call. Please continue." In some markets, you can press ★70 to disconnect the call-waiting signal before you place a call. Unfortunately, you cannot disconnect call-waiting when you receive a call. You might want to check with your service provider about other options.

As we said before, never leave a first caller for more than ten seconds to answer the call-waiting signal.

Speakerphone

Never assume it is all right to put telephone partners on a speakerphone. Don't turn it on and then expect them to object if they do not wish to be broadcast in the room. Always ask before putting someone on the speakerphone and identify the people in the room. For example: "Howard Barrow and Betty Johanon are here with me."

If you are alone and need to take notes, you can say, "I am here alone, and I need to write this down as we talk, may I put you on the speakerphone?"

Polite Ways to End a Telephone Conversation

For long-winded callers who are difficult to escape, say, "I won't take up anymore of your time. I'll get right on this project. Good-bye." (not "Bye-bye"). You can also say, "I will get back to you right away" or "Thank you for calling, Alfred" (or "Mr. Knowles").

When you can't get away from a long-winded caller using the above suggestions, tell the truth and say, "Mr. Samuels, I am alone in the office. May I place you on hold while I answer this other line? I will be right back." In these days of innuendo and outright lying, tact and truthfulness are the most important ingredients in getting off the phone without offending a long-winded caller. However, you must do this without telling the person he or she talks too much, is boring you, or is rambling about an unrelated topic. If you are pressed for time, explain that you have only a few minutes and then end the conversation when that time is up.

Some callers ramble on without getting to the point. You can say, "Mr. Salesman, I am afraid I must prepare for a meeting and have only a few minutes to talk. What can I do for you?" (or a similar question). A pleasant tone of voice is imperative, or the caller will be offended.

When callers race on without giving us a chance to speak, we have no choice but to talk over them: "Excuse me, Mr. Speedy, I don't think I am the one who can help you. This sounds like a problem only Fred

Tillman can solve. Let me switch you to his extension. It is #42. All right?" Then wait for an answer and respond with "Thank you."

Sometimes callers you don't know try the chummy approach. Perhaps they mention that a "friend" recommended you. In some businesses, if you are unfamiliar with the "friend," you can request that the caller put the proposal in writing. Insincere callers are not likely to write the letter. Their purpose may be to use the telephone to get a quick, affirmative commitment. Be aware, however, that sometimes callers we don't know simply want to make a request and they are nervous, not insincere.

When a caller has important information but is repetitive, take charge by saying, "Gene, you have your facts straight. Let me summarize the high points. We can speak again later in the week." Give the summary, then say "Thank you, goodbye."

The following additional suggestions can help you avoid being rude or telling a "white lie":

- "I wish I could talk longer, but I have to get back to an urgent project."
- "I don't mean to cut you off, but. . . ."
- "I'm sorry but. . . ."
- "It's been great talking to you, but I have to take another call" or "My next appointment is due."
- End a conversation as you would a memo. Give some indication of what action you will take. For example: "Let me work on it and I'll call you next Friday with the solution you are seeking."
- Be positive and upbeat even if you know you will not see or talk to this person again soon. You can say something similar to, "I look forward to talking to you again," or "I look forward to talking to you again sometime."

Handling Disgruntled Callers

Dealing with unhappy callers can ruin our day as nothing else can. However, when we stay calm and use a well-planned approach, we feel better even if we try but fail to solve the complainer's problems.

- We should take a deep breath and listen.
- When a caller's complaint is justified, we should take responsibility, apologize sincerely, whether it was our fault or another employee's, and tell the caller we will try to solve the problem.
- We should give callers the courtesy of listening as they vent their frustrations over the damage done by our (or our company's) error. If we are lucky, allowing them to air their grievances will satisfy them.
- We should tell callers we are writing down the major points so that we can take action to remedy the situation.
- We can tell the caller our plan to do the following:
  1. Inform everyone involved in the error.
  2. Have the principle person responsible call the customer to explain and apologize.
  3. Call back in a few days, if the caller wishes, to check on the progress of any efforts to make things right again or to report any progress in solving the problem.
- We should write the injured party to explain actions being taken on his or her behalf.

If the caller's complaint is without merit, ask him or her to please put the details of the complaint in writing so that the proper officials can study it. By the time the person gets around to writing it all down, he or she may have calmed down considerably.

It is also important to write a memo immediately to the person who might receive the complaint letter.

If the caller uses foul language, write down the words or record the conversation, if possible. Relay that information to the person in your organization who is in charge of such matters—for instance, a human resources director or the legal department.

How to Avoid Telephone Tag

We play telephone tag when we leave a message for an individual, then we miss the call back, and they leave a message for us. To avoid this unpleasant game:

- Take note of time zone differences and then choose the best time to call, such as before 11:00 A.M. and after 2:00 P.M. Call before noon on Fridays.
- If you think you know the reason for the caller's call and cannot reach him to return it, leave a message stating the information you need. For example: "If you need the exact time for the press conference today, it is noon in meeting room 4."
- Eliminate a call with a fax. When you have statistics or other complex information to convey, using the facsimile (fax) machine cuts down on phone time and reduces stress.

Returning Telephone Calls

It is good business to return someone's call who tried to return your call, even if you have obtained the needed information from another source. Briefly tell them thank you, and that you found the answer to your question in time to meet a deadline—or whatever the circumstances.

In terms of manners, we should return business calls within twenty-four hours, whether the needs are pressing or not. The failure to return calls is one of the most common complaints in business today. Even an executive who is away from the office should check in with an assistant and return the calls or make sure the assistant knows how to take care of the matter.

SERIOUS PHONE ERRORS

1. Not identifying yourself as soon as someone answers at the number you called.
2. Asking the answerer, "Who is this?" when your call is answered. (You may ask if you have reached a specific number.)
3. Saying, "Who's this?" instead of "May I ask who's calling?"
4. Putting the caller on hold without asking permission and waiting for a response.
5. Failing to confirm if you have called at a convenient time.
6. Not permitting the customer to say good-bye first.
7. Not being prepared to take notes or messages.
8. Not recording an appropriate outgoing message on your answering machine.
9. Not returning calls within twenty-four to forty-eight hours.

Delivering Less-Than-Happy News

If you must deliver bad news, do it promptly and be courteous and caring. For example, if you must report the loss of a contract, say

"Jean, I am afraid I have some bad news. Upper management has decided to award the contract to another supplier."

Handling Interruptions

Suppose someone enters your office with an urgent need while you are on the telephone. Ask your telephone mate, "Can you excuse me for a moment, please?" or say "Please excuse me for a moment." Press the mute button or cover the mouthpiece, respond to the person who walked in, then quickly return to the caller saying, "I am sorry," and go on with your conversation.

On the other hand, if a call comes in while you are conducting business with someone in your office, explain to the caller that you are in a meeting. Arrange to return the call. Never conduct a long telephone conversation in front of a visitor unless it relates to the business you are conducting with the person present.

Conference Call Manners

Conference calls save time, money, and frustration. They can expedite business deals and decisions. The business person who calls the conference begins, runs the agenda, and closes the call. He or she makes sure the expected parties are on the line and that everyone can hear adequately. Usually those present will sit around a desk or conference table, while distant participants sit near the microphone or speakerphone in an office or conference room.

The following protocol is suggested for conference calls:

- Arrive promptly and remain in the place previously agreed upon so you are ready when the call comes.
- Be patient while the participants get connected. Some of them may be in distant locations. Many people may be involved.

- Identify yourself each time you begin speaking.
- Speak distinctly and into the microphone. You may have to reposition it to do so.
- Do not interrupt while another member of the team is speaking. Talking over someone creates a jumble of words no one can understand.
- Refrain from making jokes and comments in the background. Doing so is rude and bad business.
- Remain still, keeping extraneous noise, such as moving furniture or shuffling papers, to a minimum.
- When the conference call is coming to a close, say, "Thanks, everyone. We accomplished our objective," or a similar parting word.

Using Electronic Equipment Politely

In earlier times, our mail was carried by the pony express and our messages traveled over wires by Morse code. Now we have computers that talk to each other and machines that talk to us. Yet the more technological conveniences we acquire, the more complicated our lives become. Since we cannot imagine doing business without them, we must learn to use them efficiently and politely.

Answering Machines and Voice Mail

For a business/home machine, set your device for four or fewer rings. Callers get upset waiting for more than four rings before the device picks up.

Once the machine answers, do not force the caller to listen through a musical selection or through long, unnecessary instructions before they can leave their message. They already feel annoyed at not being able to talk personally to the person they called. Record a brief message to let callers know they have reached the right number. For example, the only outgoing message necessary may be "You have reached 000-0000. Please leave your message after the tone." It is obvious that you are unavailable.

> "Hi. I'm probably here. I'm just avoiding someone I don't like. Leave me a message, and if I don't call back, it's you." (This rude outgoing message was on an answering machine as reported in *The Arkansas Democrat Gazette,* October 8, 1997.)[1]

Exception: If you have a separate business telephone line in your home, you may wish to record a new message each day stating when and where you can be reached. (Obviously, you don't want to say that no one will be home.)

If you use an automated system requiring callers to press a seemingly infinite number of choices, always give callers the option of speaking to a live voice immediately. When callers try to leave a message using a multi-button system, they often wander unsuccessfully from one option to another. Finally they hear a click and then a dial tone, which means they have reached no one. Sometimes they do not try again.

Cute messages, jokes, strange noises, and some music selections are inappropriate for an answering device in the business world. The outgoing message should be brief with only the information the caller needs.

Remind the caller to give his or her name, affiliation, phone number, time of call (unless your machine records the time automatically), and a brief message. If possible, the outgoing message should indicate when you will return the call.

My publishing company, Broadman and Holman, has a wonderful system. Each employee in the editorial department records a new message on his or her machine every morning to tell callers where and when the person may be reached. Callers are given the option of leaving a message or speaking to an assistant right away.

We should call our answering device periodically to evaluate the outgoing message for clarity and effectiveness. When the caller hears the machine message, he or she knows we are unavailable. Additional information regarding when we may be expected to return or how to contact someone else immediately are helpful to the caller.

The following suggestions are helpful when leaving messages on answering devices:

- State your name with your title and the name of your company. Even if you are a frequent caller, your name may be unfamiliar to a new or substitute telephone attendant.
- Name the person you are calling.
- Give the day and time of your call.
- Briefly summarize the reason for your call.
- Leave your telephone number, including the area code and your extension number if you have one. Even if you think the owner of the answering device knows your number, leave it anyway. It is the thoughtful thing to do.
- Don't leave a confidential message.
- Don't leave vague or mysterious messages. Practical joke messages are also inappropriate. Someone else may take the message and misinterpret your intent.
- Don't assume your message will reach the person you are calling. Machines malfunction and messages get erased. If you don't get a timely response to your call, you may wish to speak to the individual's assistant or try leaving another message.

Cellular Telephones

It is pretentious to answer your cellular phone while dining out or to have a telephone brought to the table. Restaurant personnel will tell you that you have a call and where you can take it.

> According to the Cellular Telecommunications Industry Association (CTIA) the number of wireless phone users in the United States alone was expected to exceed 60 million by the end of 1997.

Taking a call tells your companions that there is something more important than being with them or doing business with them. If you are expecting an important call, tell the other person about it at the beginning. Then excuse yourself for as brief a time as possible.

> Calls made on wireless phones are not protected by the Fourth Amendment's right to privacy. Therefore, both the government and police can legally listen in on your conversations.[2]

When calling from your car:
- Identify yourself with your first and last name when you make a call. You may say that you are calling from a car phone to expedite the call. Hint: Say, "I am calling from my car. Can you hear me clearly?"
- When you have passengers, use your car phone sparingly, if at all.

When calling from someone else's car phone:
- Identify yourself and ask if this is a good time to talk.
- Discuss only pressing issues and save other topics for office calls. Using a wireless phone is usually an expense to the owner.
- Avoid putting wireless phone users on hold.

Car phones are a valuable tool if they don't hinder safe driving. They give us immediate access to emergency assistance. We can use them to report a breakdown (our own or that of another motorist), highway accidents, instances of drunk driving, or any other unsafe driving we might see.

Alltel offers these excellent guidelines for safety:

- The safest way to use a wireless phone while driving is to use a hands-free or speakerphone.
- Employ the memory dialing functions on phones to minimize the potential for distraction.
- When dialing manually without the speed dialing feature, dial only when your automobile is stopped. If you have a passenger with you, ask them to dial for you if you cannot stop or pull over.
- Never try to take notes or look up a number while driving. Pull off the road to a safe spot.
- Let your voice mail pick up your calls when it is unsafe to answer the car phone.
- Dial your local emergency number to report crimes in progress or potentially life-threatening emergencies, accidents, or drunk and reckless drivers.
- Suspend car telephone conversations when driving conditions become hazardous.[3]

Beepers

A beeper can instantly put us in touch with one another, but it can also be the source of great annoyance if it is not programmed and used properly.

Beepers should not beep in public places. The most appropriate device is one that vibrates. The wearer can feel the pulsation and check the device for a message or telephone number to call.

For beepers that do make noise, only doctors on call or other professionals who help save lives should wear them. We should not wear them in a church, a public auditorium, a performance, or any place where other people will be disturbed by the beeping.

Laptop Computers

Always consider the tranquillity of those around you. The constant clicking of the keyboard on a cross-country flight or a long commuter trip can drive seatmates to distraction. Through no choice of their own, they feel trapped in a chamber of clatter.

Facsimile Machines

Follow the rules established in your company for using the facsimile machine. A document transmitted by fax (an acronym for facsimile) is copied by the receiver through the phone lines to another facsimile machine.

A document to be faxed should include the following: the cover sheet, the date, the name of the sender, the sender's fax number and telephone number, the name and fax number of the recipient, the page count (including the cover page), and a brief message or explanation of the faxed material to follow.

The following manners should be observed when sending faxes:

- Call ahead to inform the would-be recipient that you are sending a fax.
- Type business letters to be faxed.
- For speedy communication, rough drafts may be sent, but in legible condition only.
- Be prepared to answer questions about your faxed document by telephone.
- Send only pertinent information. Junk faxes are never welcome.

- Send only information that is not confidential or controversial. Many eyes may see whatever you send.
- Avoid using facsimile machines for an easy and quick way to send all communication. A fax is not always a substitute for the mail. Stamped, personal notes written by hand on nice paper are more appropriate for saying thanks or congratulations and for sending condolence messages.
- Respect the time and resources of the recipient of any fax. The employee or client receiving the fax must provide the paper, employee time, and the machine. Make all your faxes succinct and in appropriate good taste.
- After making a phone call or closing a sale, it is good business to send a fax for confirmation. A verbal agreement on the telephone may need to be confirmed in print.

CHAPTER 5

Business Manners for Office Staff and Guests

*A good supervisor is someone who can
step on your toes without messing up your shine.*
The Economic Press

*A good boss is someone who takes a
little more than his share of the blame and a
little less than his share of the credit.*
The Economic Press

What Is Your EQ? Office Relations

1. What are the proper manners for receiving a visitor?
2. What are the qualities of a successful boss?
3. What are the etiquette rules regarding the break room and who gets the coffee?
4. What are the proper manners for being a visitor?
5. What are the habits of every successful employee?

Good Manners in the Office

When a middle manager in a multimillion-dollar corporation barged into his boss's office to ask why he was not promoted, he was hit with an explanation that rocked him. He was told that his job performance was first-rate. The problem was his manners, his business etiquette.[1]

"Manners consultants say the new emphasis on job etiquette does not mean that you simply have more chances to do things wrong. It does mean that making the right gesture at the correct moment can boost your stock and help you stand out from the crowd."[2]

One of the first places considerate behavior should begin is with the inner office staff. Basic rules of kindness such as greeting and saying goodbye to coworkers each day are not up for debate, but some businesses require more formality than others. Each workplace has an unofficial code of behavior to fit its formal or informal atmosphere.

A relaxed, informal staff may have workers calling all employees—from the chief executive officer to the floor sweeper—by their first name. Other businesses may forbid the informality of casual-dress Fridays.

The wise employee learns to balance the rules in an etiquette book with the prevailing attitude in the office. Trying to turn an informal atmosphere into a formal one can make us appear stuffy. Not participating in tasteful humor or office parties and celebrations can make us look standoffish and rude. Yet too much frivolity and informal talk can make us dangerously unpopular, as well as make us look unprofessional.

It takes everyone in the office working together to meet the increasing demands on workers today. Being bossy never made an executive a boss. Being discourteous to the newest and lowest-paid employee reflects badly on the offender no matter how high up the pay scale they are. It also hinders the whole process of getting the job done.

A supervisor is responsible for the work his or her assistant produces. Sometimes the boss must speak to that assistant in a courteous but forceful way about poor work habits or complaints from coworkers.

The boss sets the tone for such things as showing affection. If the executive displays affection, he or she should expect others in the office to do so. As we said before, however, the safest approach in the workplace is to refrain from any physical contact except handshaking.

Shared Office Equipment

We're all familiar with that wonderful invention that breaks down, jams up, and runs out of paper at the most inopportune time—the photocopy machine. Yet most offices today can add any of a long list of new equipment that we must keep operational. The more technology we develop, the more demands we place upon employees and ourselves. Using good manners with each other as we share this equipment helps alleviate some of the stress.

If you have a lengthy copy job, yield some time to a coworker with only a few pages. If the machine needs toner or has a paper jam, correct it or tell a supervisor. When you finish a lengthy job, replenish the paper supply. According to *Agency Sales Magazine,* "Bosses and managers should refill the paper cartridges of the copy and facsimile machines when they use them."[3] No one is exempt from this courtesy.

Break Room Courtesies

Practice the following courtesies to help make break time more pleasant for everyone.

- We should use the break room and not our desk for personal habits, such as eating and chatting.
- If a "clean-up" person does the heavy work, we must at least clean up after ourselves, throw away leftovers and papers that might mold or develop a foul odor, and place used items in the sink or dishwasher before leaving.
- Unless otherwise instructed, we should unplug or replenish the coffeepot when we get the last cup.
- We should always ask before "borrowing" a coworker's snack in the refrigerator. Even if we are given permission, we should always replace it.
- Even if items are not labeled by the owner, they are not fair game.

Partitioned Office Space

To the outsider entering a large room with all available floor space partitioned into cubicles, it looks like a hopeless maze. To the one working in the cubicle, it may look and feel uncomfortably like working in a fishbowl with no privacy.

Many annoyances grow larger when there is a lack of privacy; therefore, for a noisy project such as entertaining a visitor or client, use the conference room.

Occasionally, ask the coworker in the adjoining open–plan office space if you are interfering with his or her work in any way. Don't be hurt or angry if the coworker names a few annoyances.

Truly Successful Managers

> Cooperation is doing with a smile what you have to do anyway.[4]

We sometimes think that if someone has reached the status of boss, he or she is successful. However, many subordinates will attest otherwise. Much of one's success emanates from how well a boss treats staff, peers, and superiors.

Here are just some of the qualities of a good boss:

- Cheerfully greets with a smile all employees, regardless their job status
- Calls people properly by name (and title, when appropriate)
- Never considers himself or herself "above" doing menial tasks or helping someone
- Delegates, but does not dump his or her tasks on others
- Privately and constructively critiques an employee who has made an error, no matter how insignificant or egregious
- Displays an appropriate sense of humor in the proper circumstances
- Is self-deprecating, always willing to take responsibility for errors, never placing blame on others

- Is not self-absorbed, but interested in others—an attentive listener
- Never expects employees to keep rules he or she is unwilling to observe
- Treats employees of the opposite sex as business professionals and does not require females to do the traditionally "old-fashioned female chores"

Interoffice Courtesies

Attention to others within the working environment will improve everyone's job performance.

- If a neighboring coworker's habits make your job difficult, calmly and tactfully state your objections whether you are asked or not. Proper office protocol does not dictate "suffering in silence."
- Go to the supervisor if you and the coworker cannot reach a compromise.
- Don't just "drop in" on a coworker to chat. (Hint: If you receive "drop ins" often, try delegating some of your workload to the chatterer, such as running an errand or retrieving information. You may say, "Since you are free, would you mind retrieving the fax awaiting me in the main office?").

Habits of Every Successful Employee (Including the Boss)

Adopting the following habits will improve your success no matter where you are on the career ladder.

- Always introduce people in a manner that makes each of them comfortable.
- Don't be pushy or aggressive in social situations, trying to promote your own career at the expense of another.

- Always write a note or letter to acknowledge a gift or favor.
- Be able to converse intelligently on a variety of subjects.
- Don't pretend to be a "know-it-all" on any topic of conversation.
- Know how to dress properly on and off the job—and in keeping with the company image. Seek help in building a professional-looking wardrobe if necessary.
- Never discuss private company matters with outsiders.
- Remain polite but firm with ill-mannered individuals.
- Remember that everything you do reflects on all.
- Maintain the appearance of dignity, but not superiority.
- Keep promises, obligations, and appointments.
- Always be on time. If detained, notify the host or guest.
- Return telephone calls within twenty-four hours or ask assistance in doing so.
- Don't procrastinate or neglect your duties, consequently burdening someone else's schedule.
- Return "borrowed" property quickly and in good condition.
- Don't engage in office gossip, but do attempt to stop rumors.
- Don't brag or become paranoid or defensive about your position or tasks accomplished.
- Be discreet about any personal friendships with employees or any personnel within the company.
- Give recognition and don't take credit for someone else's work.

Titles and Names to Use in the Workplace

If the atmosphere in an office is relaxed and informal and first names are the custom, certain rules apply.

When speaking to an outsider or when making introductions, use a title for fellow workers. An executive may call her assistant "Lawrence," but when introducing him or referring to him, it is better to use his position and call him "Mr. Agee, my assistant" or "Lawrence Agee, my administrative assistant" when speaking to outsiders. The assistant may call his boss "Ann," but to others he uses "Ann Madison, my boss," or "Ms. Madison, the head of the department." References to any assistant as "my girl" or "my boy" are always inappropriate and demeaning.

SEVEN RULES TO WORK BY

1. With coworkers, don't hog the credit or show an attitude of, "Didn't I do a great job?"
2. Be flexible. Don't say, "That's not my job."
3. Be humble and "make the boss feel smarter." Don't say or act like, "I already knew that."
4. Keep personal problems to yourself, telling only your supervisor when they might interfere with your work. Don't complain to coworkers with, "My personal life is a mess."
5. Dress for the position you want, but stay within the code.
6. Accept responsibility. Don't play the blame game or say, "It's not my fault."
7. Don't gossip. Example: "Did you hear how she got the job?"

Who Goes for the Coffee?

For mundane tasks such as getting the coffee or supplies, the capable, confident assistant is usually willing to assist. The executive who treats his or her assistant with dignity usually feels free to ask (not command) that individual to attend to such matters.

Such assignments may also be rotated among staff members, including the chief executive officer. No one in the office should be too important to get the coffee, select gifts, or arrange social events.

Communicating to Management about Coworkers

When is it appropriate for an assistant to tell the executive news about a coworker? It is permissible only when it is work related or when job performance is at issue. Otherwise, the news is simply gossip. For instance, when a coworker is engaged in illegal or unethical activities, the executive should be told.

Business Hosts and Visitors

When guests enter our offices we should greet them pleasantly and in a timely fashion, just as we would welcome them into our homes. We want their first impression of the staff and surroundings to be warm but businesslike.

Reception Area Protocol

Visitors, including those coming for a job interview, should observe the following rules of proper conduct in the reception area.

- Be on time.
- Check your appearance just before entering the business.
- Approach the receptionist and identify yourself by name and company, stating your reason for being there. Present your business card, which you have in hand before you enter.
- If you are a few minutes early, acknowledge that fact and state your willingness to wait, not wishing to intrude on your host.

- Thank the receptionist after your conversation.
- Remain standing until you are told where to sit.
- If there is no coatrack, fold your coat over your lap. Your demeanor and conduct while you wait shows you to be either businesslike or amateurish. The executive you await may quiz the receptionist later about your behavior.
- Keep your posture erect at all times. If you sit on a plush chair or sofa, don't sit back. If you attempt to stand to your feet when someone approaches you and then fall backward, you appear inept and juvenile.
- Remain quiet. Don't fidget, make noise, ask unnecessary questions, scramble around in a purse or briefcase, or attend to any grooming needs, such as clipping your nails. All these misdemeanors are noticed and leave bad impressions.

Office Protocol

The following suggestions help establish a good impression when the receptionist finally says, "He/she will see you now."

- Rise when an assistant approaches to usher you into the executive's office. Keep your right hand free to extend it for a firm handshake once you enter the host's office, and state your name to the executive if the assistant neglects to introduce you.
- Remain standing until the host sits or asks you to be seated.
- When you are seated, follow the host's lead and be prepared to spend three or four minutes in small talk.
- Don't slouch or appear too relaxed. Stay focused.
- Be sensitive to your host's time commitments. If you scheduled the meeting, you may ask how much time he or she can spend.

- When it is time to leave, stand simultaneously with the executive/interviewer, thank your host, shake hands (women also), and exit.
- Make a positive statement such as a desire for the position.
- Be cordial to the assistant and others who may glance up as you leave the office.

Receiving a Visitor

As the host, you should observe the following protocol to make visitors feel welcome and at ease.

- Be as gracious as you would in your own home.
- Visitors or clients entering a business or office should never be left standing awkwardly, waiting for someone to address them.
- Both female and male employees should rise and move from behind their desks to greet clients, visitors, and senior executives (but not inner office personnel who may enter or exit often). Switchboard operators who also serve as receptionists are not required to stand, but should acknowledge visitors as soon as they enter. Eye contact and a smile are imperative.
- The receptionist should keep the visitor informed about efforts being made to meet his or her needs (such as how much longer the wait will be).
- Confident hosts introduce themselves as they extend their hand, even if they assume the visitor knows their name.
- The perfect host always anticipates any immediate need of the visitor when he or she enters, offering refreshments when available. The hosts says, "Can I get you coffee, a soft drink, or water?" (These may be offered in the waiting area by the host's assistant.)

- The host takes the guest's coat, suggests a place for the visitor to sit, and exchanges some pleasantries before proceeding to business.
- The host employee (from the receptionist to the CEO) should listen attentively to visitors' requests or stated purposes.
- To put guests at ease, the host executive may choose to sit in a chair adjacent to the visitor instead of behind the desk.
- When the meeting is over, the host stands, extends his or her hand, and thanks the visitor for coming.
- If the host must end the meeting early, he or she may apologize for an imminent engagement or appointment.
- The host escorts visitors and clients to the door of the elevator and makes sure they know how to get out of the building. Another employee may be asked to do this if the host is needed elsewhere.

CHAPTER 6

Packaging Yourself: Dressing for Business

The critical factor in credibility is presenting the expected image. . . . Don't wear anything that will surprise the people you meet in business.

John T. Molloy

What Is Your EQ? Business Attire in/out of the Office

1. What is proper attire for today's workplace?
2. What are the taboos in business dress for men and women?
3. What does "business casual" mean?
4. What does "black tie" for a business-related event mean?
5. What are the criteria for buying a business suit?

During the past thirty years a virtual revolution in thinking has changed the way we dress up or down for work and for business/social functions. Twenty-five years ago a woman who wore a pantsuit or a man who wore no coat and tie were not welcome in nice restaurants.

In the office, men wore three-piece suits and women wore similar business suits. Our choices and decisions were easier because they were limited. Today the slippage of tailored business attire is a growing trend—even a downright landslide.

Many employees are understandably dazed and confused as to what is appropriate and what is not. The starch has gone out of many workplaces. It started with casual holiday evenings and events staged to raise funds for charities. Then only Friday was the "dress down" day. Before long, some workplaces had gone to daily casual wear.

Entire books and magazines are available on how people should dress to go to work, however, much of that information is based on the assumption that everyone works in a nine to five office job where only the brain works. Today's workplaces are far too varied to place everyone in that category. Some jobs require physical agility. Some people work outside in the weather, some with the public, and some in secluded labs, seeing only coworkers during the day.

Some occupations of respected workers who do not wear three-piece suits to work include: utility workers, mail carriers, airline attendants, vehicle mechanics, animal trainers, country music performers, police officers, nurses, doctors, greenhouse nursery owners, gym personnel, aerobics instructors, produce growers, assembly line workers, grocery clerks, beauticians, and barbers. Few if any of these occupations require a business suit. We like it when workers give us no surprises, appearing as we expect to see them.

Case studies over the years have proven that credibility and professionalism are the critical factors in getting a job and in being promoted whether we are in the public eye, doing research, or reading the water meter. We have to dress and look the way most people expect that we should, regardless of the rigors of our job.

People believe that they have a right to wear whatever they please, but the reality is that at work other people have to look at them and customers must transact business with them. Customers can take their business elsewhere, but coworkers can't simply walk away.

The way we dress should be a matter of common courtesy and respect for the sensibilities of others. We have about sixteen hours between workdays and forty-eight hours on weekends to exercise our right to dress freely.

> "The key is to present no visual surprises."[1]

The way we dress is not the only determining factor in the image we present, but dressing inappropriately or in a nonprofessional way usually doesn't leave an impression of success, competency, or trustworthiness. It may affect our salaries, our move up the career ladder and our tenure.

Since the seventies, women have greatly improved their credibility and acceptance in a predominately male workplace. Most women no longer feel they have to wear male-type clothing to the office to be successful. Today a conservative dress with a jacket or blazer is most often seen.

The critical point to remember is that image is very important. For example, in one company, an employee with superb abilities presented too many surprises in attire each morning. Company executives asked me to take this individual shopping, with the company paying the tab.

Because occupations vary widely let's first look at some general guidelines for business attire based on research and experience. We will then narrow our focus to give more specific suggestions according to job type, gender, and circumstances.

Dressing for Business

Much of corporate America has peeled off its dark business suit, loosened its power tie, and kicked off the high heels to go casual. About 85 million of the 118 million employees in this country are dressing down for work. As many as 90 percent wear casual clothing occasionally, according to research done by the Dayton Hudson Corporation.[2] Workers anchored to their computers, eating lunch beside the PC mouse, don't always need to wear the traditional business suit.

For generations, however, the only office apparel allowed consisted of "the suit," a tie, and the starched shirt that could stand on its own. Though casual dress is now being assimilated into America's workforce, corporate casual has not yet been fully accepted.

Casual dressing does not work in some positions, and not all casual wear is created equal. For example, people in lending institutions, banks, and other areas of finance as well as many other jobs require a more disciplined look. The clients and customers they do business with expect to see the sellers, buyers, and lenders look successful, as though they pay attention to detail and have the discipline and respect to dress that way. Clients don't want to entrust their life savings, legal matters, and business affairs to people who appear sloppy or too relaxed.

The correct business look is not just for those who make big decisions and earn big paychecks. Personnel directors often base their first impression of applicants on clothing, grooming, and accessories, even when the job description does not require a suit and tie. For instance, one employment agency tells job seekers who come in wearing cutoffs and sneakers or leggings and a sweater that if they want to succeed, they must dress for the job they want, not the position they formerly held.

> "You want the audience to concentrate on what you're saying, not on what you are wearing."[3]

The businessman who chooses a well-fitted suit and a conservative, silk tie (or a navy blazer and gray or beige trousers in some offices) is saying, "I'm here to do business in a cooperative and competent manner—whatever that takes."

What is more, many people feel they perform best when dressed up. An account executive in the Southwest, whose two biggest clients are on the East Coast, communicates with them by telephone and fax. She never sees them in person, therefore she does not wear the traditional business suit to dial their number. However, she says,

"I don't do jeans because I don't feel businesslike in them. If I am really dressed down, I don't feel confident even doing business on the telephone."

The trendy businessman who wears a zoo print tie, sports jacket, and trousers in clashing colors may be saying, "I'm creative. I do things my own way," but his appearance limits his potential (unless, perhaps, he is in the field of entertainment or the arts).

Fads and Fashion Versus Style

Fads and fashion are a multimillion dollar business, as changeable as the four seasons. Trying to keep up with them can ruin our budget, as well as our business appearance. It is easier and wiser to follow the business dress code.

Like it or not, the standard for proper attire in the business community does not change much. The executive wardrobe includes clothing in classic styles. There is little room for personal preference and taste, at least in the broad sense. Although personality can be displayed through carefully chosen accessories, men find it is better to be remembered for their competence than for their flamboyant ties; women, for their abilities rather than their costume jewelry.

Skills, expertise, and competence are the marks of a professional. Conforming and blending in may not be the most comfortable choices, but they are essential for the workplace. Whether the CEO or a school teacher, we must look the part. Our business image must fit our job description. A crucial component in forming that perception is the way we dress for work—our professional attire.

Employees may conclude that because no one comments about their appearance, they must be appropriately dressed. The sad truth is that if a superior calls attention to something about an employee's appearance, it has been bothering the boss for months, and others have been talking. The damage to one's image may be irreparable.

Those who take offense at the notion that what they wear is almost as important as what they know should realize that "those who dress to fit in, get ahead," as one executive told me. It is essential to project the image that will please those in authority, those who ultimately control our professional destiny.

The following list consists of some of the inappropriate aspects of appearance actually observed by businesspeople in their workplaces. The list is not intended to be unjustly critical or a reflection on the individual's character—the items are simply inappropriate for most jobs.

- chewing gum
- toothpicks or matches
- the geeky or grunge look
- clothes that ride up
- pants that drift downward
- clothes with the "slept in look"
- culottes
- stretch pants
- sequin-studded T-shirts
- strapless sundresses
- sneakers
- crop tops
- bare midriffs
- men wearing earrings
- women with too many earrings
- athletic shoes

- biking, golf, and jogging shorts
- cutoffs
- frayed shorts
- short shorts
- tank tops
- shirts with offensive messages or graphics
- loud-colored plaid sports coats
- scruffy-looking work boots
- see-through clothing
- plunging necklines
- dark hosiery with a white skirt
- spandex
- windsuits made of parachute material
- platform sandals that slap the floor

- heels spindly as needles that dent the flooring
- skirts dinky enough to be a scarf
- slits in skirts that are more like slashes
- slips of the wrong color showing through the slit
- high heels that wobble and stumble
- lingerie-type clothing
- chiffon or after-five dresses
- go-go boots
- blue denim jeans
- overblouses that reveal bare midriffs
- unlined pants that reveal the wearer's underpants
- ankle-high hosiery with a skirt
- a ring on every finger
- men in white socks and dress shoes or bobby socks with business suits

The list goes on.

Some employees assume that if their clothing and accessories cost enough, they are automatically judged to be correct. However, expensive clothes that are wrinkled, poorly fitted, or in the wrong colors for business make a negative statement.

Projecting a Professional Image

Let's examine some specifics for those in the corporate world who believe traditional attire makes them more credible and effective in their jobs.

Men

Appropriate business dress will vary from company to company, industry to industry, and even from region to region throughout the country. For instance, dress in Los Angeles or Denver tends to be more casual than attire worn Boston or New York. Learn the code for your profession and dress accordingly. You can usually watch those who are successful and experienced.

The Business Suit. Buying a business suit can be a big investment. It is wiser to buy only a few suits of good quality rather than many cheap ones. Assuming you will shop for the most expensive suit your budget will allow, your first consideration should be quality and fit.

Business suits are available (1) off the rack (usually the lowest priced), (2) semi-custom (medium-priced), and (3) custom (most expensive). Beyond the price tag, the difference in the three may lie in the amount of special alterations the store offers.

In good stores, off-the-rack suits may be a good choice if the store offers you a first fitting and alterations at no cost. Suits with such amenities are worth any extra money you pay to get one of quality and fit.

With a semi-custom suit, you can select the fabric swatch and style of tailoring details. This kind of suit will come with several alteration fittings for the perfect look, even on a man who is hard to fit.

A custom suit will cost more. The salesperson in such a shop will usually know all that is necessary to be well-dressed for business.

Good Grooming and Attention to Details. Even a high-quality suit is cheapened by poor grooming and lack of attention to details. To polish your professional image, attend to the following guidelines:

- Shirts (except those with button-down collars) should have stays in the collars.
- The dress code for each change in seasons in your area must be followed. (For instance, light, corded suits are inappropriate in the winter except in California or hot-weather climates such as Florida.)
- Outfits (if only the tie) should be changed each day.
- White socks are never worn with a business suit.

- Riding or hunting boots should never come to work.
- Hair should be clean, neatly combed, and appropriately short.
- Shoes should be well polished, with sole dressing applied.
- Shoes that lace (wing-tip or cap-toe) or loafers with a tassel are best in business. Color should be black or cordovan.
- Jackets must be pressed and well fitted.
- A tie should reach the belt, not above and not below it. (Silk ties are best.)
- A suit should be of wool, wool blend, or silk—not 100 percent polyester. Suits with 25 to 40 percent polyester do not wrinkle as easily as wool, but they are hotter than 100 percent worsted wool. Worsted wool is usually tropical or summer-weight wool.
- Suit colors may include gray, charcoal or navy (light brown or tan in the summer).
- Suits, shirts, socks, or ties of loud patterns are not usually appropriate.
- Trousers with a cuff are preferred.
- Shirts should be white or light blue. Striped shirts are usually appropriate only in quiet, muted stripes. Men in conservative businesses usually are more restrained in their business attire, wearing only white or blue shirts and subdued ties.
- Shirt collars must be large enough to button easily at the neck. You can't hide a gaping shirt collar under the tie.
- Socks should leave no exposed skin between the trouser cuff and the shoe when a man sits or crosses his legs. Only mid-calf length socks are usually long enough.

Business Casual Wear for Men. Unless they work outside, deliver the mail, or work in construction, men (and women) should save shorts for nonworking hours.

The following should be minimum requirements for business casual:

- shirts must have collars, such as high quality golf shirts
- button-up shirts with collars, but no tie are also a good choice
- with the exception of the company logo or slogan, caps and shirts should be free of all captions
- no shorts, jeans, or sneakers with holes are appropriate

Convention and Conference Attire. Sometimes at national business meetings or conventions it may be difficult to know what clothes to pack. However, many organizations send a tip sheet regarding weather, climate, scheduled events, and appropriate attire. For meetings in resort areas dress is less formal, but never the "ragged jeans, or jeans with holes or fringe and a loose sweatshirt look." Boots, sneakers, and athletic shoes with holes are taboo.

If you have no way of knowing the correct attire, dress in a suit and tie the first day. Then observe the style other colleagues of your position, or higher, wear and dress accordingly. If you get to the meeting and feel inappropriately dressed because the other men dress casually, you can always remove your tie and suit jacket (and vest if you are wearing one).

Weekend and Out-of-Town Work with the Boss. If you will be working with superiors, ask what attire they will be wearing. Then choose the same style. If casual clothes are recommended, be sure yours are neat, clean, and appropriately expensive for business.

Women

After thirty years of research, John T. Molloy in his book *New Women's Dress for Success*, writes, "When a woman dresses for success, it does not guarantee success, but if she dresses poorly or inappropriately, it almost ensures failure."[4]

Molloy goes on to say that in interviews, "improper dress is the most common reason job candidates are eliminated."[5] When asked to keep a list of qualified people who were turned down and the reason for their rejection, interviewers gave "image" as the reason in 40 percent of the cases.[6] A woman's appearance seems to be more important than a man's, especially if she is interviewed by a woman. Three times as many women are turned down for jobs because of how they are dressed.

(Molloy suggests that a female job candidate try to find out if a woman will be interviewing her. If so, she should attempt to dress similar to her interviewer, whether suit or dress, casual or traditional.)

One reason women are judged more harshly is that, unlike men, when women "wear an outfit their superiors think is totally inappropriate, no one tells them."[7] Because women are in a minority in the workplace, management is often afraid to tell a woman she is inappropriately dressed.

Another reason is the fashion/fad trap. Molloy says women should ignore the high-fashion industry because it does not serve the businesswoman well. Designers are continuously looking for changes they can make in the market; therefore, tradition and the best business attire do not serve the designer's need to sell.

Although fashion writers tell women that a woman's position has changed in our society and that they should wear the latest styles to work, research proves that the latest fad-fashion look is a liability in more traditional jobs. Women are entering a far more competitive world than those of their mothers or even their older sisters. Like men—maybe even more so—they need to learn the code and dress accordingly.

The Jacket. The jacket is for women what the business suit is for men. It has become the hallmark of the American businesswoman.

In over 90 percent of the cases tested, the jacket indicated authority, rank, power, and professionalism, even when worn with a dress. In fact, a very tall woman is advised to wear a jacket/dress in place of a suit.

So what kind of jacket are we talking about? A blazer is a lightweight jacket, usually cut to the top of the thigh. The better ones are always lined, which provides a more tailored and structured look.

The very short jacket is called a bolero and is cropped above the waist. It is worn open in the front and usually with a matching dress. The bolero is named for a Spanish dance featuring castanets.

The most effective blazer-type jacket usually hangs ten inches below the waist and looks more businesslike than it does sexy.

The best fabrics for a blazer are linen, silk, wool, or wool lookalike. Not all, but most tweeds have a sporty look.

The Conservative Business Suit. "It works," say hundreds of women. The fashion industry tried to stamp it out in the late 1980s, but because of its high-authority impact, it remains a staple in most wardrobes of business attire.

Women have gone from the openly aggressive and somewhat masculine styles of the '70s to the quietly assertive, feminine styles of today. Although popular, red is not a good color for women in business. It may give the women a feeling of power, but it sends the wrong message.

The Shorts Suit. In some offices in various parts of the country, the shorts suit is acceptable. Some people call them "walking shorts." Whatever the name, they are shorts with a jacket of the same high-quality fabric. The shorts reach almost to the knee, and they must be worn with hosiery and flats. The price tag is usually as much as a regular business suit.

Make sure the jacket and shorts are the right proportion for your figure, covering what they should. They do not flatter or look professional on large women with heavy legs.

The Dress. The best colors for dresses in business are deep blue, navy, tan, beige, medium blue, grayish brown, dark brown, and dark gray. Again, red is not good.

The best fabrics are wools, gabardine, and blends of not less than 50 percent wool. Tweeds are acceptable if they have a substantial look.

If a woman's size is too intimidating, she may wear a dress to diminish it, that is, if her job does not call for a look of intimidation.

Avoid any material that is sexy, clingy, rides up, or wrinkles easily.

Hosiery. Flesh-colored hosiery is best. Black and navy blue are acceptable with a matching dress or skirt, but only on young, thin women. White, patterns, and designs are bad hosiery choices for business.

Shoes. Low to mid-heel pumps with closed toe and heel are the best choices. Avoid white. The shoe color should complement, not strongly contrast with, the color of the skirt.

Business Accessories. To look professional a woman's briefcase and purse should not look like a matched pair. They should have understated hardware on genuine leather. The best colors are brown, beige, black, and navy. If lighter-colored handbags are carried in the summer in your area, buy beige or light tan instead of white. Solid colors are favored over patterns.

These accessories, along with a notepad and pen, are always in view and can make a statement about a woman's success. Spend as much as your budget will allow for visibly high quality. Well-chosen accessories will serve you for a long time.

Business Casual for Women. The new buzzword in the workplace is "refined casual." It suggests a trend away from "distressed casual" to "professional casual." The distressed casual (the worn-out, tattered look) does not carry enough professional weight. The key to dressing professionally even on casual days is to remember that it is not Saturday casual but business casual. It is somewhere between the career suit and Saturday "grubs."

To maintain the professional look, many women shop in the women's department of the most conservative men's store. They look for the same color combinations and fabrics as the better-dressed men's casual wear.

Colors announce our status, effectiveness, attitude, and credibility. Loud, flashy colors in business casual for women are as bad as they are in traditional business attire.

Experienced businesswomen don't try to cut down on cost by thinking casual should be less expensive. They spend comparatively as much on their business casual wear as they do on their traditional business clothes.

Tip: Keep a loose-fitting cardigan sweater and a navy blue jacket in the office. If you wear a conservative suit to the office and need to dress down to casual, you can replace your jacket with a loose-fitting sweater. When you need to go from office casual to business dress, you can put on the navy blue jacket.

Men usually wear traditional golf clothing on casual days. Women may do the same. Bad choices, however, include jeans, short shorts, culottes, stretch pants, and the like. If your work calls for pants, choose those that are full-cut, loose (not baggy), and in a dark, solid color.

Women in Labor-Intensive Jobs. For women in labor-intensive jobs, denim is acceptable so long as it is not blue denim, according to John Molloy. It can be dyed khaki, beige, brown, or black when the men wear blue jeans. These women usually stay away from pink, lacy, or frilly garments while at work.

Attention to Details in Grooming. In the best interest of the businesswoman, most successful business professionals recommend the following:

- Blouses should be made of silk, silklike polyester, or cotton. White or off-white are good choices.
- Skirts should be no shorter than one to two inches above the knee.
- Jewelry should not stand out (such as a ring on every finger).
- Strong colognes, scented powder, and perfumes, if worn at all, should only whisper, not shout.
- Hair should always be neat. If you have long, below-the-shoulder length hair, it should be pinned up for doing business. "Long hair over your shoulders sends a sexual message to . . . men. As a result, it makes you less effective. . . . It sets up an unprofessional relationship between you and . . . men."[8]
- Makeup should be subdued and natural. Nails should be manicured, not too long, and never polished in bright colors or decorations.

Recreational Attire Outside the Office. For a business/social event the invitation may simply say "dress casually." Without more information, we often have difficulty knowing what that means. Some party goers say that means silk they must send to the dry cleaners. For others, it means a Chambray shirt, jeans or khakis, and new sneakers.

The type of fabric often defines how sporty or dressy a garment is, especially one with a pattern. If you are not sure what fabrics are appropriate by name, visit a fabric store and ask for assistance in identifying them. For instance, most of us know about denim and velour, but what about seersucker, sail cloth, gabardine, chiffon, or 100 percent polyester?

Usually, the proper dress varies from place to place. If you are new to the area, ask a trusted friend with experience.

If the event is business related, you must look your best to maintain a professional image.

Recreation and Parties in Business

Business may not always be serious work, but business is always serious. Office parties in the office or in a restaurant or hotel require business attire. The office party may appear to be entirely social, but it is not. In a way, we are still working and we should dress in formal wear, business attire, or business casual. If the party is on a weekend or after 8:00 P.M., the setting may be less official, but what we wear should be in good taste to show we are serious about our career.

Receptions and Dinners

The invitation, whether written or spoken, should make it clear whether an event requires formal dress, business dress, or business casual. If it does not so designate, you may ask, "How should we dress?" or "What is the dress for this event?" Sometimes you can base your decision about proper attire on the event and location, but it is safer to ask.

Business Dress for the Evening

At an evening event when the invitation says, "Business Dress," that means the men are to wear a dark blue or black business suit, a white shirt, and a silk tie. The women are to wear a business suit and blouse with low to mid-heel pumps or a tailored dress (never frilly, lacy, or revealing). A dress with a jacket is often a better choice than a dress alone. The jacket remains on throughout the evening.

If the invitation says, "Black Tie Optional" (which is too broad) ask someone, or wear a tuxedo. If the man opts for a tuxedo, his female partner of such an invitation will wear an after-five (cocktail) dress. The hemline comes to mid-calf.

Formal Attire

Formal wear is worn in the evening. It may be required for a ceremony, an awards banquet, a holiday party, or an evening at the theater, all of which may be business related. Formal dress is inappropriate for the office.

For men, "black tie" means black patent shoes, a black tuxedo, and a black, hand-tied bow tie with a white, starched, studded shirt.

"White tie" on the invitation is the most formal attire required of men. It means black patent shoes, a white tail coat and trousers, and a white, hand-tied bow tie with a white, starched, studded (instead of buttoned) shirt.

A tail coat is short to the waist in front with long tails in the back and is required for only the most formal occasions. Few business-related events require such formality.

Businessmen should never wear loud, decorative ties, cummerbunds, or ruffled shirts for any formal occasion. High school prom goers often wear them, but they are not the best choice, even for young men.

For women, "black tie" means a soft dress with sleeves and a long, narrow skirt. Understated elegance is always best. Wearing short or mid-calf dresses (sometimes called cocktail dresses) to black-tie events is popular in some areas, but where tradition is respected, wear only a long dress. Ask about the local custom if you are unsure.

"White tie," for women, means her most formal attire. She should wear an elegant gown with some shoulder treatment. Do not wear a strapless gown. Marjabelle Young Stewart, an etiquette expert, tells about the time she wore a strapless dress (before she knew better). The woman sitting on the other side of the table told Ms. Stewart that she looked naked.

The Importance of a Dress Code

Many corporations have adopted dress codes or have amended policies to deal with the casual businesswear issue. A long list of taboos may not be necessary. The code may vary from company to company or from business to business, but employees need to know what is expected. Most people are uncomfortable seeing a clerk at the hardware store in a crop top baring her midriff, and we lose our appetite when a waiter with tattooed hands and a nose ring serves our food. Perhaps you or a committee of employees can use the information in this chapter to make a simple list of expectations to fit your particular business.

The way someone dresses may not be a reason for dismissal, but if guidelines are in place when the person is hired, employers can avoid regretting they hired that employee. Sometimes the way an applicant dresses for the interview is not their usual business dress.

As the writer of the code for your business, you may feel like a crotchety old "stick in the mud," but policy makers should make clear when they hire people what kind of dress is considered appropriate. A worker's dress reflects what he or she thinks of himself, the business, and the customer—be it respect, indifference, or disrespect.

The intent of a dress code is to discourage people from dressing so outlandishly that the only thing customers or clients remember about doing business with an employee is what he or she was wearing or not wearing.

To test your professionalism, look in the mirror before you leave for work and ask yourself if you are dressed appropriately—not too trendy, not too comfortably, not with the look of a "carefree weekend," but properly projecting a professional image. As Molloy says, "Don't let your clothing get in the way of business."[9]

COMMON *FAUX PAS* IN PROFESSIONAL APPEARANCE

Men

Wearing a limp shirt or inappropriate shoes with a suit.

Wearing short socks that expose the skin when the legs are crossed.

Wearing one's jacket unbuttoned. (Exceptions: sitting or wearing double-breasted)

Wearing unpolished shoes or shoes needing repair.

Wearing a tie too short, too long, or too gaudy. It should not detract from the business discussion. Clients need to remember the man, not the tie.

Poorly groomed facial hair (beard, nose, ears, or brows untrimmed).

Chewing gum or using a toothpick in public.

Women

Wearing too many accessories.

Undergarments showing.

Skirt shorter than one inch above the knee.

Being over- or underdressed.

Hair longer than shoulder length (unless pinned up).

Chipped nail polish.

Grooming in public.

Too much makeup.

Open-toed shoes.

Patterned or colorful hosiery.

Dressing for fad or current fashion rather than for style and good taste in business attire.

Chewing gum or using a toothpick in public.

DEVELOPING A BUSINESSWOMAN'S WARDROBE

Budgeting

- Take inventory each season. Hang together clothing you can wear during the current season. See how many outfits you can put together. Assess items that need to be updated (for instance, a new white or beige blouse)
- Decide how much you can spend

Questions to Ask When Shopping

1. What articles in my closet will go with this?
2. Is it of good quality? Check seams, hems, lining, zipper, etc.
3. Is this on my "needs assessment list" and in my budget?
4. What type of care will it require? Dry cleaning or hand washing?
5. Will it need alterations?
6. How long will it be in style? Animal prints, stirrup pants, square-toed shoes, and twist-a-bead necklaces are examples of fads that come and go.
7. How many times a season can I wear it?
8. What is the exchange or refund policy of the store?

With the following formula, decide how much an article will really cost you:

1. How many times could you wear the garment in a week?
2. Multiply that by 50 (or weeks in the season).
3. Divide the price of the garment by the number of times you could wear it.

The answer reveals how much the garment will cost during a season or a one-year period. A faddish skirt that cost fifty dollars could cost you five dollars each time if you can wear it only twice a month during a season.

CHAPTER 7

Person-to-Person
Introductions

*Introducing people is one of the most important acts
of business life, yet very few people know
how to do it right.*
Dorthea Johnson

What Is Your EQ? Making Person-to-Person Introductions

1. What is the most important rule in face-to-face introductions?

2. What are my options if I forget someone's name?

3. How do I introduce my boss and a customer?

4. How do I introduce a man and a woman in business?

5. What are the rules for introductions in a receiving line?

Politicians are experts at it, but no matter how hard some of us try, we stumble, or worse—we avoid making person-to-person introductions altogether.

How do the candidates running for office do it? How do they remember all those names? Do they know something or have something we don't? Not really. With desire and practice they have mastered the techniques, which all of us can learn.

Their secret lies in having an incentive, an innate desire to make other people comfortable. Their future to elected office may depend on how well they handle their interpersonal skills. Making introductions and remembering names rank high on their list of important business manners.

The Art of Shaking Hands

Before we discuss the how-tos and what-not-to-dos of introductions, let's look at a basic component of most introductions, especially in business—shaking hands.

Three rules of thumb for introductions and shaking hands are:

- Address authority figures first and introduce others to them.

- Men and women should stand and shake hands when introduced, regardless the status of the person they are meeting.
- Always shake hands when meeting someone for the first time, at chance meetings, and for all farewells.

Handshakes are important because they take some effort, and they communicate our friendliness. All women and men in business should shake hands (except those individuals who have both hands physically impaired). The following guidelines show the proper way to shake hands:

- Shake hands by meeting the web between your index finger and thumb with the web of the other individual's hand.
- Use a firm, but not crushing, grip. Do not use a limp, fishlike grasp, but use a lighter grip if the person has visible arthritis.
- Shake hands with a gentle up and down motion. Don't pump, and don't clasp too long. Businesspeople usually shake hands until they finish greeting one another by name. Shake at least as long as it takes to say, "Hello, Mack" and the other to say, "Hello, James."
- Go ahead and shake a proffered left hand (the right hand may be impaired). You may want to clasp the left hand from the side.
- Shake hands the best way you can when others extend their fingertips, with the palm turned downward. Sometimes you can gently guide the hand into the proper position.

The Business Rules for Person-to-Person Introductions

The most important rule in making introductions is: *make them*—even if you don't remember the formal rules or can't recall the names.

Introductions in the business world are based on pecking order. Authority takes precedence over gender; that is, the person of lesser status is introduced to the person of higher status or authority— regardless of gender. In the social world introductions are based on age and gender. (See "Social Rules for Person-to-Person Introductions" later in this chapter.)

The Standard Method

The following steps are involved in all business introductions.

Step 1. Decide who is the most important in terms of seniority and present him or her with "a gift" of the less important person.

Who are these "more important people"? They are customers, clients, distinguished guests, dignitaries, senior staff members or executives, and people in authority. In terms of importance, most executives prefer that customers and clients be given the place of "most important."

Step 2. Address the senior ranking person first. In other words, look at the person as you call his or her name: "Mr. Important, I'd like to introduce Mr. Less Important, our new associate" (the words *to you* are implied).

Step 3. Then turn your attention to the other individual: "Mr. Less Important, this is Mr. Important, our section leader."

While mastering the above technique, use the same steps and the wording you feel comfortable with until you become a pro. The following guidelines will also help you fine-tune your skill:

- Look at the person who needs the information, not at the person whose name you are saying. Each individual needs to hear the new name, not his or her own name.
- It is not kind to command people: "Mr. Jones, shake hands with Mr. Jacobs."

- Don't repeat the names like a bouncing ball. For example, it is not good to bounce the names to and fro, "Ms. Jones. Ms. Smith," then turn and say, "Ms. Smith. Ms. Jones."

The only time double introductions are appropriate is when the noise level is high, such as at a ballgame, in a receiving line, or at a large party.

Specific Examples

Introduce your peers from another organization or business (if they are not customers) to your boss.

"Mrs. Graves, this is James Brown, a salesman for Remco Steel."

Turn to James Brown and say, "Alice Graves, our department manager."

Introduce your boss to a customer.

"John, (customer) I'd like to introduce our division manager, Dr. Sam Gaddis."

Turn to Dr. Gaddis and say, "This is John Evans from Kelso, Inc. He accepted our invitation to the demonstration today."

Remember, potential customers are usually more important than in-house employees. Most executives prefer that the customer or client be given the place of importance.

Introduce same-level associates within your company to peers from another company.

"Jeanette (peer from another company), I'd like to introduce Mary Aspen, who is in charge of our warehouse."

Turn and say, "Mary, this is Jeanette Dawson, vice-president of Associated Products."

Introduce a junior executive to a senior executive.

"Ms. Senior Executive, this is (or I'd like to introduce) our new receptionist, Carl Bates."

Turn and say "Carl, this is Margaret Angler, head of our marketing department."

Introduce a nonofficial person to an official one.

"Senator Horne, this is lobbyist Keith Laman."

After stating the names, we must also give the new acquaintances some information about one another so they can carry on a conversation. We can name their positions, what company they represent, or perhaps, how we know them.

What to Do When You Are Introduced

Extend your hand, say hello (or something similar), and repeat the new acquaintance's name. Talk a while before excusing yourself from him or her.

The Social Rules for Person-to-Person Introductions

Socially, the rules are based on age (younger to older) and sex (male to female).

"Mrs. Williams, (older) this is Jenny Allen (younger)." Notice that the older person's name is stated first, because you are introducing a younger person (the gift) to an older person.

Turn and say, "Jenny, this is Mrs. Williams."

When introducing a male to a female, say, "Ms. Harvey (female), this is Mr. Samuels (male)."

Turn and say, "Mr. Samuels (male), this is Ms. Harvey (female)."

If Mr. Samuels is much older or is a dignitary, you will introduce Ms. Harvey to him: "Mr. Samuels, this is (or I'd like to introduce) Ms. Harvey."

- Usually we introduce a family member to an "outsider" even when we are not in a host/guest situation; however, we may introduce a young friend to a parent or grandparent. We simply make a personal judgement about who should be honored, then call that name first and present the gift (of the other's name) to that individual.

- Students introduce their parents to a school teacher and other school officials.

- In both formal and informal social introductions the first name spoken is that of the older or more distinguished person. The second name is that of the person being presented (as a gift). Socially, men are presented to women, unless the gentleman is a dignitary.

- According to international diplomatic protocol, women are presented to ambassadors, ministers in charge of legations, chiefs of state, royalty, and dignitaries of the church. You would say, for example, "Mr. Ambassador, may I present (or this is) Mrs. Ames."

When responding to an introduction simply say, "Hello, Mr. (Ms. or Mrs.) Samuels." Then you can say more, but it is imperative to repeat the person's name to help you remember it and to establish if you heard the name correctly.

General Information About Introductions

When No One Introduces You

Have you ever stood awkwardly wondering if someone was going to introduce you? Most of us have. If this happens to you when you are among people who know one another, wait for a pause in the conversation and introduce yourself.

If you are in friendly surroundings and are seated next to a stranger for any period of time, introduce yourself by looking at the person and saying, "Hello. I'm George Nickels." Make a comment, and the new acquaintance may or may not choose to engage in conversation.

If the other person is standing, rise, smile, step forward, extend your hand, and state your name. Shake hands and repeat the person's name when you hear it.

When You Forget a Name

Have you ever forgotten a person's name? One of our biggest fears is forgetting someone's name. Even the fear of forgetting further paralyzes our memory.

When you can't recall a name, try the following techniques before admitting you have gone blank. One of them usually works.

- Extend your hand and introduce yourself to the newcomer even though you are sure she knows you. Say, "Hi. Sarah James from Alco Corporation," or "Hello, I'm Sarah James. We met at the convention in Denver last year" (if you remember that much about the person).
- If it works, the newcomer will say, "Hello. Tom Eckerman from Seattle. How are you?" (He may not remember your name either; therefore, it is always a courtesy to give your name to spare someone a possible embarrassment.)

When we see someone struggling to remember our name, we must never make a game of it, by saying, "You don't remember me, do you?" or "It starts with an *S.*"

What if nothing works and you cannot get the name out of the newcomer?

- Remain calm and just admit you can't remember it by saying something such as: "I know we have met, but I simply cannot recall your name," or "Today I can't seem to remember my own name," or "I'm having trouble remembering names today. Help me out."

If we don't blurt out, "I don't remember you," we won't offend someone. All of us have been in that awful predicament; therefore, we understand.

- When introducing others and you go blank you can say: "I'm terrible with names. Why don't you introduce yourselves" or "Help me out and introduce yourselves." Although this is the least desirable option, we do have a responsibility to see that our friends and acquaintances in close proximity get to know one another. It is better to do it all wrong than neglect to try. Not to introduce people makes the newcomer to the group feel left out; the others feel uncomfortable; and we look unprofessional and insensitive.

Ways to Remember Names

To avoid the embarrassment of forgetting names, try these methods to improve your memory.

- When the name is spoken, concentrate on the person and the name you want to remember, not on yourself and your fear.
- Use the new acquaintance's name often in conversation to retain it in your mental computer.
- Visually write the name on the person's forehead.
- Associate the name with something about the person's appearance. If the woman's name is *Jill Hilleson*, you may remember her by the old expression: Jack and *Jill* ran up the *hill*. (This does not work for me because I tend to call the new acquaintance by the association I made with the name. If a woman's name is *Ringer*, and I associate it with *bell*, I will likely call the woman *Mrs. Bell* instead of *Mrs. Ringer*.)

One of these methods should work for you. Still, be alert and try to avoid embarrassing mistakes. For example, in one community there are two prominent surnames that are very similar, at least in meaning. They are *Pigg* and *Hogg*. An account executive in one of my classes told me that he calls on both contractors to solicit their business. Unfortunately he once called *Mr. Pigg* by the name *Mr. Hogg*.

What if you must give up trying to remember the person's name? Do not pretend to forget to introduce the two people. It is always better to admit that you can't remember a name than to ignore the courtesy owed to friends and colleagues.

When to Use First Names

Never assume that you may call someone by his or her first name. If you have any doubts when addressing someone, such as when meeting or greeting the individual, use the last name. It is important to use a title (Mr. Mrs. Ms. Dr.) before the last name. The person you address formally can always say, "Oh, please call me John."

Perhaps you call your boss Jerry. When "outsiders" are present, you should still use a title with his last name and let the boss say, "Please call me Jerry."

How to Manage Group Introductions

When introducing one or two people to a group of five or more, simply state the name of the newcomer and ask the others to introduce themselves. They should do that at a convenient time during the day or evening.

Responding to Mispronounced Names

When our name is mispronounced, we should kindly correct it one time. After that, we may have to endure answering to our mispronounced name.

If your name is mispronounced during an introduction, wait until the introducer is finished. As you greet the new acquaintance, simply say, "It's Tom."

Clarifying Misunderstood Names

If the introduction was unclear, simply ask the individual to repeat it or say, "I didn't quite get your name." People like to have their name spoken correctly. They prefer that we ask for a clarification if we are in doubt.

When Introductions Are Unnecessary

You may avoid introductions in the following situations:

- If you pass someone on the street or in the hallway, it is not necessary to stop and introduce those with you.
- If people briefly stop by your restaurant table, you usually do not introduce them unless they stay a while to chat.
- If a group stops by your table you can bypass introductions (or follow the advice given in "How to Manage Group Introductions").

When a Married Woman Uses Her Maiden Name

- When a married woman uses her maiden name in business, we introduce her as Alice Horne even though socially she may be Mrs. Robert Allen. If she is with her spouse, we can say, "This is John Smith and his wife Alice Horne." Otherwise, the living arrangements are not mentioned.
- If a surname is hyphenated, use both. Melinda Bryant-Heath will be Ms. Bryant-Heath.
- If a married woman uses her maiden name in business, she must make certain that her husband is introduced properly.

The country-western singer, June Carter would say, "I'm June Carter, and this is my husband, Johnny Cash." If someone calls him Mr. Carter, Johnny or June should say, "It's Mr. Cash."

Introducing a "Significant Other"

The only appropriate and safe word to use in this situation is *friend*. If you are introducing a man and his girlfriend to someone named Sarah Miller, simply say, "Sarah, this is Harry Mason and his friend, Connie Watts."

How to Say Good-bye After an Introduction

Just before you walk away, it is always a good idea to say a word or two to someone you have just met. For example: "It was nice to meet you after all this time," or "I hope to see you again," or something similar. If you say, "I've heard so many things about you," be sure to add the word *good*: "I've heard so many *good* things about you."

When Introductions Are Inappropriate

When a speech or some other activity is in progress, it may be inappropriate to talk. Simply nod to acknowledge the person and take care of introductions later.

Avoid the Use of "Insider" Names

We may call our sister Mary, but others call her Dr. Mary Alder. The name we use for a relative or acquaintance may not be the name the new acquaintances will feel comfortable using. We call these "insider" names. They are not appropriate in making introductions.

If we call our boss by her first name, we should introduce her as Susan Kirk, chairman (or chairperson) of our board.

Avoid the Use of Nicknames

In the executive office most pet names and nicknames do not portray a businesslike impression of the individual. The shortened form of *William* is *Bill*, which is acceptable, but *Smooze, Spanky,* and *Bubba* are not.

I have a friend we called by the nickname *Spanky* all through college, but when he became an investment adviser, his friends were glad to change to *Bill*, short for *William*. Few of us would trust our IRA to *Spanky*, but *Bill* became a success.

The main reason for using formal names and titles is to avoid putting the new acquaintance in an awkward position. He or she may feel uncomfortable calling the new acquaintance *Junior* or *Sis*.

Introductions at Group Functions

Receiving Lines

When there are forty-five people or more, the guests may not personally know the hosts or one another. Since guests usually mingle before an event, a receiving line is helpful for introductions so that further conversations are less awkward.

- The first person in the receiving line turns to the second person and introduces the guest. They shake hands. After these two introductions, the guest proceeds down the line giving his or her name and company name to each person in the receiving line.
- After you think most of the guests have arrived, the staff greeters and the host may leave the line to mingle among the guests, taking care to watch for any latecomers.

- The line should be near the entrance, but not in an area that can become crowded quickly, such as near a staircase or near the refreshment table.
- It is proper but not mandatory that spouses stand in the receiving line. However, if the honored guest's spouse does so, then the host's spouse stands in it also.
- A staff member should alert the host if the waiting line is getting too long. He or she can suggest that things move a little faster to avoid an uncomfortably long wait for the other guests.
- If there are several hosts, they can take turns standing in the line to meet guests.
- The members of the receiving line should not hold their refreshments. If necessary, they may place a beverage on a nearby table, getting a sip between guests.

No Receiving Line

- When there is no receiving line at a large function, at least two staff members should make sure everyone who arrives is introduced to the host. The host and at least one of the introducers must remain available, preferably near the entrance. Neither the host nor the staff introducers can retreat to a corner of the room with a favorite guest and neglect his or her duties.
- A staff member must also introduce each guest to one or more guests who can carry on a conversation with that incoming guest.
- The host, the staff members, and the guests should keep their right hand free to shake hands as they are introduced. That means holding a beverage in the left hand so the right hand will not become wet and cold, and you will not need to juggle the glass to shake hands.

CORRECT FORMS OF ADDRESS

Position	Introducing or Addressing an Envelope	Speaking or Writing To
American Ambassador	The Honorable Carl (Carla) Bale American Embassy	Ambassador Bale
Governor	The Honorable Carl (Kay)Hanks Governor of New Jersey	Governor Hanks
U.S. Senator	The Honorable Gus Bream United States Senate	Senator Bream
State Senator	The Honorable Joe Barnes	Senator Barnes
Mayor	The Honorable Sam Lassiter Mayor of Richmond	Mayor Lassiter
U.S. President	The President The White House	Mr. President
The First Lady	Mrs. Hardwick	Mrs. Hardwick
(no first name—only one woman can be the presiding first lady)		
Lawyer (men)	Mr. Al Kempner★	Mr. Kempner
(female)	Ms. Ann Kempner★	Ms. Kempner
Member of the Clergy	The Reverend James (Jane) Pate, The Reverend Dr. James (Jane) Pate	Mr. (Ms.) Smith Dr. Pate
Rabbi	Rabbi Marvin (Mary) Qualls	Rabbi, or Rabbi Qualls
Secretary	Ms. Alice Koe	Ms. Koe
State Representative	The Honorable Mary (Al) Marks	Ms. (Mr.) Marks
U.S. Representative	The Honorable Jack (Sue) Ames House of Representatives	Mr. (Ms.) Ames

★ If (Esq.) is used after the name, omit the *Mr. (Mrs.)* before the name.

SOCIAL INTRODUCTIONS

The most important rule: You must *always* introduce people.

Basic Rules:

- A younger person is always introduced to an older person. Say the name of the older person first.
  Example: "Aunt Sarah, this is my friend, Kim."
  "Kim, this is my Aunt Sarah Fillmore."

- A person is introduced to someone of a higher position or rank.
  Example: "Mrs. Johnson, this is my neighbor, Mrs. Paul."
  "Mrs. Paul, this is Mrs. Johnson, our principal."

- A man is presented to a woman and a boy to a girl.
  Example: "Mrs. Watson, this is my father, Mr. Green."

- Males stand when being introduced to a female.

- Gentlemen always shake hands with other males.

- Gentlemen wait for a lady to extend a hand. If she does not extend her hand, the gentleman does not extend his. (*In business,* either the male or the female may extend a hand first.)

- Forgotten Names: Everyone forgets sometime. Just admit it and move on.
  Example: Look at the person whose name you cannot remember and say, "I have just gone blank. Could you help me out?" The person then says his/her name.

- Correct response when you are introduced: "Hello, Sammy." or "Hi, Sammy." Always say the person's name. It will help you remember it.

- Introducing someone to a group: "I want all of you to meet Alicia Fowler from Omaha. She is new in our school." Everyone should introduce themselves to Alicia after that. With a *small* group, you can tell her each person's name.

THE MOST COMMON *FAUX PAS*
IN MAKING INTRODUCTIONS

1. Failing to introduce people.

2. Remaining seated when meeting someone.
   Exceptions: (a) when the other person is seated, and (b) when it is difficult to rise (such as when seated in a booth). In this case, nodding or placing one's palms on the table as if to rise is acceptable.

3. Offering one's fingers instead of hand; giving a "fish handshake."

4. Wearing a name tag on the left.

5. Neglecting to repeat a person's name when introduced to him or her.

6. Failing to offer your hand in a business situation (especially women failing to do it).

CHAPTER 8

Business Dining

The world was my oyster, but I used the wrong fork.
Oscar Wilde

What Is Your EQ? Dining with Clients and Colleagues

1. What is the proper procedure for arranging a luncheon or dinner engagement with a client? What about canceling one?
2. If a guest is late in arriving at the restaurant for a dining engagement, how long should the host wait?
3. Do you know what to do if you or your client prays before a meal?
4. What is the difference between American and European styles of dining?
5. What is the proper way to refuse food or beverage?

Today, our largest social environment is found in the business community. A rapidly expanding global economy forces us, more than ever before, to socialize and conduct business while we eat.

In this setting we acquire and develop business relationships—old ones and new ones. The best and worst place to make a first impression is at the table. Even the most educated among us must be trained in the social graces to succeed in the business world.

No one wants to dine and do business with someone who has not learned to wield a knife and fork, use a napkin when needed, and swallow a bite of food before speaking. Even those at nearby tables notice our table manners—or lack of them.

How we put food in our mouth is a major part of our professional and social image. Even if we don't slurp our soup, others who know enough to break off a pinch of a roll will cringe when they see us chomp into a big roll to get a mouthful.

Lack of table manners is simply one more signal to others of our level of experience and polish in people skills. Business executives who have already made it to the top frequently languish over the lack of social polish in those who are to follow them.

> John Kennedy, Jr., his sister, and their mother were invited to the White House for dinner. John, Jr. was very young and during dessert he spilled milk all over President Nixon's lap.
>
> The former president's son said, "He [President Nixon] didn't even blink. He just wiped it up and I kind of just died slowly in the corner."
>
> President Nixon showed what it means to be a gracious host.

The rules of dining have a purpose and are not difficult to master. Some of the rules are for safety. The others are to keep us from "grossing everyone out," as one of my young students put it.

Some examples of safety are holding and placing our silverware properly and not waving it around in the air, poking ourself in the eye with an iced teaspoon handle that we left sticking up in our glass, or flipping our soup spoon across the table because we left the handle protruding upward in the bowl.

Knowing what to do and when to do it relieves nervousness, thereby freeing our minds to concentrate on the business before us. Whether we are the host or the guest, we want to be at ease in business and social circles. Whether we dine with two courses or seven, we can be spared painfully embarrassing mistakes.

Pre-Dining Etiquette

Whether you are combining business with dining to keep a loyal customer, make new business contacts, or to thank someone for a favor, planning is everything.

Protocol for the Host

The host is the man or woman who arranges the business meeting around a meal. The duties of the host involve every minute detail of the dining situation from extending the invitation to making the reservations, to leaving the tip, to paying the check, and finally to retrieving a coat from the coat attendant.

To be a confident host you must follow some guidelines. To be a host who is remembered, you must really care about the needs and comfort of your guests. Whether you entertain a businessperson at a backyard barbecue or at a formal ball, your kindness, consideration, and attention to detail will make a big difference. Your guests will remember your caring attention and demeanor more than the Bananas Foster at the end of a seven-course feast.

To make your guests comfortable you must see that they are introduced to other guests, that the food is tasty, and that conversation flows naturally with no one feeling left out. You'll even want to make sure the bathrooms are clean. (A man can ask a woman coworker to check out the ladies' bathroom in a particular restaurant before making a reservation. A businesswoman can ask a male coworker to do the same.)

Making the Arrangements

Choose a restaurant you trust where the staff knows you. You will feel in control and your guest will enjoy seeing you greeted by name.

If you are in your client's home territory and not your own, arrive early at the restaurant, introduce yourself to the maître d', select the table, and familiarize yourself with the surroundings and the menu.

Maître d' is short for maître d'hotel in French. It means "master of the house."

You may want to ask the management to imprint your credit card and hold the check for your signature after the meeting. The maître d' can discreetly present the check for you to sign as you leave the restaurant.

The Invitation

Extending an invitation to lunch is a better choice than dinner for conducting business. You should extend an invitation to a business dinner only when you know someone well and have a good business reason to meet after 6:00 P.M. Never invite someone to a business lunch or dinner without a reason or an agenda.

To extend the invitation, it is best to place the call yourself, especially for a first-time invitation.

The Location

The host selects the location for the meal. He or she never asks a guest where they want to eat. The host may ask if the guest has a preference or any dietary restrictions. The location should be convenient for the guest.

Choose a place where you think your client will feel comfortable, taking into consideration the ambiance and formality of the restaurant. If you are returning an invitation, you should attempt to entertain in a similar manner.

Smoking or Nonsmoking

After the two of you have agreed upon the date, time, and location for the meeting, ask your guest about choosing the smoking or nonsmoking sections. If the guest says, "Smoking, please," you should honor his request. If you are allergic to smoke, let that be known before you ask: "I have terrible allergies. Do you mind if we sit in the nonsmoking section?" Wait for an answer.

Making the Reservations

Make the reservations at the restaurant in your name and in the name of your company. The receipt should reflect that this is a business meal.

Choose a table that will give you maximum privacy for conducting business. It should not face a mirror or be near the kitchen or restrooms.

Reconfirm your reservation the day before the meeting. Then confirm the date, time, and location with your guest.

For a breakfast meeting, make confirmations the afternoon before. Also, for early morning meetings, give your guest your home telephone number to call in case an emergency arises. If the meeting is canceled, call the restaurant. You don't want to be known as a "no-show."

At the Restaurant

Arrive at the restaurant at least fifteen minutes early. Locate the table and determine its suitability. Make arrangements for paying the check. Taking charge early leaves no doubt among restaurant personnel or anyone else that you are the host.

If you must arrive late, call the restaurant and ask the maître d' to seat your guest and inform him or her that you will be detained briefly. Ask the maître d' to serve the guest a cup of coffee or a cold drink.

If the guest is not on time, wait about fifteen minutes before calling to see if there is a problem. If you are unable to reach the guest or an assistant by telephone, you must wait at least thirty minutes past the agreed-upon time. Then you may either order and eat or leave. (Even if you do not eat, you must leave a tip for taking one of the server's tables for a time.)

While you wait at your table for the guest, do not order anything to drink or pick up your napkin. You don't want your guest to think he or she has inconvenienced you in any way. Stand as your guest approaches you, and remain standing until he or she is seated at your table.

If you have waited in the foyer of the restaurant, allow the guest(s) to follow the maître d' to your table. He should seat the guest first, preferably facing the room. If there is more than one guest, indicate their places and do not sit until they are seated. The seat of honor for the ranking guest is on the host's right, however sometimes that is not practical.

As soon as everyone is seated comfortably, the host lifts the napkin and unfolds it in half. A man places it over one leg with the fold toward his knees. A woman does the same, except she places it across her lap with the fold toward her knees. (See page 135)

Ordering the Meal

Make small talk for a few minutes before requesting a menu. Don't bury your head in the menu. Talk through it with the server and ask about house specialties.

Always put your guest at ease by suggesting something on the menu or indicating what you plan to order. The guest may have no idea about the limitations on your expense budget. To clear up any monetary confusion, suggest one of the appetizers and a more expensive entree. (If time or your budget is short, you may choose not to suggest an appetizer.)

Allow your guest to order first. If the guest does order an appetizer and an expensive entree, you should order similar, though not necessarily, the same food.

As the meal progresses, pay close attention to the needs of your guest. Observe and occasionally ask your guest if he or she needs anything. You are responsible for signaling the server to bring more water, bread, or anything else.

If problems arise, be businesslike with the server, speaking in a normal tone of voice. Say, "Please" and "Thank you." Do not express anger about the food. The server did not prepare the food; he or she just delivered it. Speak directly to the maître d' about any major problems when you are out of your guest's presence.

If your guest's food is not prepared properly, politely ask the maître d' to return it for necessary corrections. The host should eat very slowly, or not at all, while the guest sits waiting for his food to return.

Taking Care of Business

After the orders are given, the host may move the conversation toward business matters. Plan to discuss only one or two items, not a long list of topics. Listen attentively, asking questions when necessary.

Be quick to say so if you don't have specific information. Say something such as, "But I will find out and get right back to you on that." Establish a trusting rapport with your client.

If time allows, encourage your guest to have dessert. If your guest chooses coffee but no dessert, you should decline dessert also. If the guest orders dessert, you should do the same.

In America we say, "Check, please." In France, it is "L'addition, s'il vous plait." In Spain, it is "La cuenta por favor," and in Turkey, it's "Hesap, lutfen."

The Check

When coffee and/or dessert are served, request the check if you have not made prior arrangements for payment. Use your credit card.

Post-Dining Etiquette

Respect your guest's time and be prompt in closing the meal. Don't linger by allowing the conversation to stray onto irrelevant topics.

Check the bill for accuracy and the tip, but do not haggle over the math. Any discrepancies should be settled out of your guest's presence, if possible. Whatever the error, always be calm and businesslike in settling the matter.

The Tip

The tip is supposed to be a reward for service performed.

It also supplements an employee's income. The word *tip* comes from an innkeeper's sign "To Insure Promptness." When customers deposited a few coins, they received their drinks or food faster.

Tipping is voluntary, but expected in America. The average gratuity is 15 or 20 percent of the total bill (before taxes). Some restaurants add the gratuity into the total before presenting the check to you.

If you learn that you are the guest of the restaurant for whatever reason, you must still leave a tip for the server of that table.

At formal restaurants the maître d' receives ten to twenty dollars in cash, depending on the size of your group. When you shake his hand upon leaving you may discreetly deposit the tip.

The person taking your order should receive 5 percent of the check. The server then gets 15 percent of the check, which is divided among all those involved in serving you, including the bussers who clear the table.

To simplify the whole matter you can leave a generous tip of 20 percent and let the restaurant manager handle the matter. You may also add 20 percent to the tip line of your credit card voucher.

When the host is female and the guest is male, sometimes a male guest will insist on paying the bill. The businesswoman in charge will say, "You are the guest of XYZ Corporation today, and they are treating us to lunch" or something similar. By giving such a response, she removes the gender issue without embarrassing the guest.

The Option to Stand

A man always has the option to stand when a woman leaves or returns to the table, but most businesswomen do not expect this courtesy at a business meal. The host does not stand for a man to leave or return to the table, unless he is a most distinguished guest.

Leaving the Restaurant

Escort your guest to the door. Take care of the coats you may have checked with the attendant. Leave one dollar for the first coat and fifty cents for each additional coat or item left with the coat attendant.

Outside the restaurant shake hands and thank your guest for joining you for the meeting. Say you will look forward to your next meeting, or say that you will call in a few days.

Protocol for the Guest

Thank the host, commenting favorably on the restaurant and the food. Write a thank-you note as soon as you return to your office, if possible. Under no circumstances should you wait more than a few days to write.

Writing to say thank you is always preferred to saying it by telephone. Sending a fax or e-mail as a thank-you note after dining is not a good choice. If no one can read your handwriting, you may send a typewritten note.

In your note, be specific, if you can, about the proposal or purpose of the meeting. Write a note even if the host was asking for your business.

You may write a few words on a correspondence card or fold-over note, but make it professional. Slip it into an envelope with the front of the note facing you. Then mail it promptly. Note the following example:

> Ms. Satterfield (or Martha, if on a first name basis),
> We had a good meeting today, and I enjoyed the lunch we shared at Montrell's. I look forward to receiving your proposal on our joint venture. Thank you.

Leave a blank line and sign your first and last name on the right-hand side of the paper. Use no titles before or after your signature.

Proper Etiquette in an Upscale Restaurant

A full-service restaurant usually has a hostess or maître d' to seat you. Tablecloths may cover the tables and the check is often brought to you at the table.

If you are the guest, watch the host for all cues, doing as the host does.

Before sitting down, introduce yourself to those around you and greet other guests that you already know. Then you will begin the evening with a feeling of calm. You will look forward with assurance to the entire experience.

If there are place cards, sit where yours indicates. Never rearrange place cards. They are placed with thoughtful care according to protocol.

Being Seated

Move to the right of your chair and enter from your left. Sit down on the front of the chair without extending your derriere. Men pull out chairs for women, and the women say thank you.

Professional women do not expect this courtesy. If a man is in doubt, he may make the offer. She will usually accept. If not, she may reach for the chair herself.

Sorting Through the Puzzle of Tableware

You may have a maze of forks, knives, spoons, glasses, and dishes in front of you. Don't be nervous. Usually, the tableware is set for practical use.

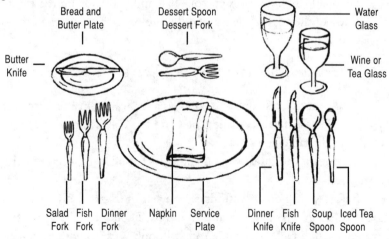

Formal Business Dinner

Forks: The Anglo-Saxons used forks as early as the seventh century. Then the religious rulers said they resembled the devil's pitchfork, and they disappeared for several hundred years.

In 1633 King Charles I of England used a fork and it never disappeared again.

Silverware. The first pieces of flatware to be used should be in logical sequence. We work from the outside moving inward toward the plate as we progress through the meal. Flatware is arranged logically and in the proper order for us to use.

Occasionally the table is improperly set, such as when the soup spoon lies on the inside next to the plate and the soup is served first. Simply use common sense. For instance, we never eat steak with a spoon.

Remember that servers sometimes bring the necessary dining pieces when they bring the dish containing the next course. If you suspect the table setting is incorrect, or if you don't see the logical utensil for a course, watch your host.

Knives and the soup spoons will be on your right with the forks on the left. The seafood fork is the only fork you ever find on the right side of your plate. Sometimes the tines of that tiny fork will rest on the bowl of the soup spoon, but it may be presented on the plate when the seafood course is served.

The custom of serving the salad before the entree (main course) originated in California to appease hungry, impatient diners. In other parts of the world the salad is always served after the main course and before dessert. The term "salad California style" refers to this new custom.

(When traveling abroad, your salad will likely come after the entree. If it does, your salad fork will rest next to the plate between the plate and the dinner fork. The knife will be on your right.)

The dessert fork and spoon appear above the dinner plate, or you will find them on either side of the plate, adjacent to it. Sometimes they are brought with your dessert. (When the meal is so formal that the salad is served after the entree, the dessert pieces will either be at the top of the plate, or they will be brought when the dessert is served.)

If you pick up the wrong utensil, simply go on eating with it and ask the waiter for another one before the next course.

Glasses and Cups. Glasses and cups are always on the right. Glasses arranged in the order they are to be used are placed above the knife and soup spoon. The water glass is always placed above the tip of the knife. This beverage is nearest the center at the top of your plate. The iced tea glass is on the right of the water goblet.

Use the other glasses in the order they are placed. Begin with the glass farthest to your right. Each glass is removed as you finish the course assigned to it. (Occasionally, the server will bring the glass when he or she brings the beverage.)

The Plates. When you sit down, the only plates you will likely see are a bread and butter plate (top left) and the service plate (sometimes called a charger) directly in front of you. Service plates are quite large. Your courses will be brought in individual dishes and placed on this plate. Your service plate will be removed immediately before your dinner plate (entree) is brought.

The B & B (bread and butter) plate should be on the left above your forks. It is a good depository for paper wrappings and even small finger foods. The B & B knife is smaller than your dinner knife. If you have one, it will rest across the top of the B & B plate. Remember, the three words *bread, butter,* and *above* all have *B*s in them.

In truly formal meals the salad is served as a course, however at banquets we often see the salad plate on the table when we sit down. If so, it will be to the left of the forks.

The Napkin. Finally, there is the napkin. In nicer restaurants the napkin is often decoratively folded and placed in the center of your service plate. Other places for it are to the left of the forks or beneath the forks.

The Dining Lesson

The most formal meal available in any part of the world is the dinner with five or more of the following courses: soup, fish, sorbet, a main dish (entree) of meat or fowl, salad, dessert, and coffee. You can master it with a little practice. Then you should feel confident in any dining situation.

First, the host directs everyone to take their seats. The guests should move to the right side of their chairs and enter from their left.

The Napkin

As soon as everyone is seated, the first step in the protocol of restaurant dining is not ordering the meal but lifting the napkin. In many upscale restaurants, the maître d' will drape a napkin in each diner's lap.

If the host sees that this restaurant does not perform that ritual, he or she should pick up the napkin, unfold it, and place it on his or her lap.

Both men and women leave a large dinner napkin folded in half as they place it on their lap. Men drape a napkin over one leg and place the folded edge of the large napkin toward the cuff of their trousers. Similarly, women drape the napkin across their lap with the folded edge toward the hem of their skirt. Small luncheon napkins are opened fully onto your lap or leg.

To use the napkin once your food arrives, reach toward your knees and lift the napkin by its folded edge. After dabbing the corners of your mouth with it, replace the napkin in your lap. Any smudge or stain will then be exposed on the outer side of the napkin and will not soil your dress or trousers.

The napkin remains in your lap until you get up to leave the restaurant. If you must leave the table for any reason during the meal, simply place the napkin loosely to the left of your plate. Retrieve it when you return. (Some etiquette instructors say to drop the napkin in your chair when you leave the table temporarily, but you risk getting food or grease on the chair seat and then on your clothing.)

The Silent Pause

After ordering and receiving the meal, the host should always give the guest the opportunity to pray before dining. Often a silent pause is all that is necessary. Individuals in business have told me that in their role as host they were embarrassed when they continued talking, only to look up and see their guest with his or her head bowed in prayer before the meal. The host may also quietly announce that it is his or her custom to pray before a meal: "I always like to say the blessing before eating," or "I know you won't mind if we bow a moment before we begin."

Serving the Meal

The rules for serving have remained traditionally the same since the late 1800s. For both left-handed and right-handed individuals, food is served from their left and each course is removed from their right. Instructions for dining are always given for the right-handed person. If you are left-handed, simply reverse the instruction when necessary, but don't rearrange the place setting.

To help you remember, think of the letters *L* and *R*. Lower from the left. Remove from the right.

Beverages are poured and glasses cleared from the right. Glasses and cups remain on the table while the server fills them. Nothing except your lips should ever touch the rim of a glass.

If the sugar or artificial sweeteners are within your reach in front of you, pick up the container, take what you need, and pass the container to your right. You may wish to offer it to the person sitting next to you before taking one for yourself. Once you begin the container's passage around a large table, you may never see it again to serve yourself.

Everyone at the table should do the same with any condiments they see in front of them. If you need the salad dressing, for instance, and no one passes it around, simply say, "Please pass the. . . ." Then the container should be passed to you by the shortest route, regardless of the direction.

Preparing the Beverages

To prepare a beverage with sugar or an artificial sweetener, tear open the package and empty the contents into the glass or cup. Gently fold the paper and place it on your bread and butter plate or on the plate beneath the glass or cup.

If you use lemon, cover the wedge with your left hand and squeeze it with your right hand. You may choose to drop the lemon wedge into the glass or cup and press it with the iced teaspoon to release the juice, being careful not to make noise. The iced teaspoon is the one with the longest handle.

Place the spoon on the underlying plate. If there is no plate under the iced tea glass, invert the bowl of the spoon and prop it on another plate. The iced teaspoon is the only utensil you will ever prop. Also, you may place the wet bowl of the teaspoon on another piece of flatware. If you replace the spoon on the table, the tea will permanently stain the cloth.

The courses in formal dinners do not necessarily come in the same order; however, the sorbet must be served immediately before the entree to cleanse the palate.

American and Continental Styles of Dining

From this point onward, the diner will eat using either the American style or the Continental style of dining. Both styles are acceptable. As Americans, we are the only diners in the world who shift our knife and fork from hand to hand while eating. For that reason, it is called American style.

From the caveman days people have put food in their mouth with their right hand. It was not until a few short centuries ago that Europeans began to eat with what we now call the Continental style (inverted fork in the left hand and knife in the right). The upper class changed to the Continental style to make a class distinction between the rich and the poor. Soon all classes of people ate that way. That was when etiquette was considered snobbish.

Americans continue to eat the original way, in part because the change in Europe came about as our country was being settled.

The American Style. The fork is held in the left hand and the knife in the right hand. After cutting a bite of food, put the knife down and exchange the fork from the left hand to the right. The American

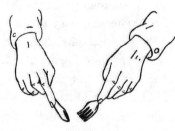

Hand Positions for Cutting

Used by permission from Dorothea Johnson,
Director of the Protocol School in Washington.

Incorrect Cutting

Correct Cutting

Correct American

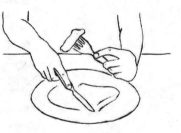

Correct Continental

diner holds the fork like a pencil in the right hand and gently spears the morsel before placing it in the mouth.

The Continental Style. Today, the Continental style is used by the rest of the world and by many Americans. The fork is held in the left hand with the tines down. The index finger is placed on the spine of the fork. The knife is held in the right hand with the index finger on the dull side of the blade. The somewhat pointed end of the knife handle pushes into the palm of the right hand.

The knife is used to cut food and to help push food onto the back of the fork. There is no shifting of utensils. The diner continues to hold the knife in the right hand while placing the fork, tines down and laden with food, into the mouth.

> Using a knife to cut lettuce was once a no-no because the vinegar in the salad dressing would discolor the knife blade. That was before we had stainless steel.

The Soup Course

Hold the soup spoon like a pencil with the handle between your index finger and middle finger. The thumb will secure it on the top. Dip the soup away from you with the spoon in a horizontal position.

Soup spoon usage

Incorrect   Correct

Move the bottom of the spoon across the back of the soup bowl to remove any excess soup that might drip. The bowl of the spoon will point to your left. Sip from the side of the spoon without making noises.

If there are handles on the bowl, you may tip the bowl away from you to get the last of the soup with the spoon.

When resting, sipping your beverage, or using your napkin, place the spoon on the little plate beneath the bowl—never in the bowl. This will prevent an accident with a protruding spoon handle.

The soup is sometimes presented in a shallow soup plate with wide rims. You may then place the spoon horizontally in the bowl with no fear of a mishap. It is very difficult to place the spoon between the rim of a soup plate and the service plate beneath it.

The Salad Course

When the lettuce is properly prepared in the kitchen we don't need a knife. We can leave it on the table while we eat the salad with only a salad fork.

Unfortunately, we sometimes face what looks like a whole head of lettuce. A knife is essential. In a properly formal setting, we find a salad knife on our right; but often this is not available and we are forced to use the only knife we see—our dinner knife.

When we must use it for anything before the entree, we should rest it on the bread and butter plate when we finish the salad, otherwise the knife will disappear with the salad or later with the service plate. Do not place used silverware back on the tablecloth.

If you lose your dinner knife, ask a server to please bring you another.

If the salad is served with cheese, use your knife to place a small portion on your salad plate. Then use a knife to spread cheese on one cracker or piece of bread at a time.

When you finish eating the salad course, place the salad fork and salad knife (if you have one) in the "finished" position (see page 144), even if you used only the fork.

The Fish Course

Fish is usually baked or grilled and served either in portions or as a whole fish. Fish should be eaten continental style.

The fish knife and fork are easy to recognize. The placement of the fish fork on the left will correspond with that of the fish knife on the right. The knife has a wide, dull blade with a notch on the top near the tip of the knife blade. You will find light indentations on the

Using fish knife to flake the fish

tines of the fish fork. They are for lifting the skeleton of the fish when it is served with bones.

Fish Served in Portions. To eat fish served in portions, hold the fish fork in your left hand, tines down. Hold the fish knife like a pencil (this is different from the method described on page 138 for a dinner knife). Steady the knife between your pointed index finger and curved middle finger. The knife handle should rest on the web between your thumb and index finger.

Use the fish knife to flake the fish and guide it onto the backside of your fork tines. Fish is tender; therefore, it should be flaked, not cut as you would a piece of meat.

If you choose to eat only in the American style, you may use the fish fork alone. Leave the knife on the table and hold the fork in your right hand with the tines up. When you finish eating the fish, place both the knife and fork in the 10 to 4 position.

Each handle will extend about an inch over the rim of the plate. Never gangplank the fork and knife with the ends of the handles resting on the table.

Fish Served Whole. The notch on the fish knife is used to separate the halves of a whole fish. When fish is served whole, use the notch to separate the top and bottom halves.

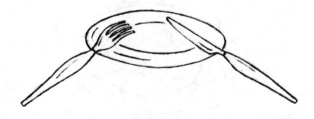

Fork and knife gangplanked

Secure the fish with the inverted fish fork. With the knife, remove the edge of the stomach. Repeat the process along the backbone. Lift away the top half. You now have a portion of fish. Eat it as described above.

As you eat the fish, remove any small bones from your mouth with your thumb and index finger. Place them on the side of your plate or on the plate provided for bones. When you finish eating the fish course, place the fork and knife in the "finished" position (see below). The only time we may put our fingers in our mouth is to retrieve a fish bone.

After eating the top filet, slip the knife between the other filet and the backbone. Lift away the backbone and place it on the side of your plate or on the plate provided for bones. Then you may eat the remainder of the fish.

The Finished Position for the Flatware

Imagine your plate is the face of a clock. Place the knife in the 10 and 4 position with the cutting edge of the knife facing the center of the plate. The tip of the knife should point to 10 and the handle to 4.

Place the fork, tines down, parallel to and just below the knife. The handles will extend toward the lower right-hand side of the plate.

Finished Position

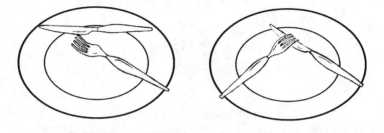

Resting American   Resting Continental

The Resting Position for Flatware

Use the "resting" position when you lay the fork and knife down to pause or take a sip of water. Think of this position as an inverted "V."

Continental Style. Cross the fork over the knife on your plate with the tines of the fork pointing downward and toward the 2 on your clock face. The handle will point to 8. Remember, the fish fork was in your left hand so that is the way you lay it down.

American Style. The resting position for the American style is to simply lay the fork on your plate as you are holding it, not in the 10 to 4 position however.

The resting position is a universally known silent signal to show that the diner has not finished eating that course. Unfortunately, not all restaurant servers know about silent flatware signals. If a waiter attempts to remove your plate, simply say, "I have not finished."

The Sorbet Course

Sorbet is frozen fruit juice and contains no milk solids. It is a palate cleanser served in a compote or dish on an underlying plate. It is always served immediately before the entree.

Sorbet resting/finishing position

A small spoon will be on the underlying plate when the server brings this course. Leave the spoon on the plate when you are resting and when you finish. You may use your left hand to steady the compote or dish.

Eat the sorbet as you would ice cream. You may remove any drips from the spoon by moving it across the rim of the compote, similar to the way you eat soup. The garnish may be eaten or left on the underlying plate.

The Entree (Main Course)

A dinner knife must be held properly for cutting meat or fowl. Do not hold a dinner knife the same way you hold a fish knife. For both American and continental style, the method of cutting meat or fowl is the same. The end of the knife handle should point into your right palm. Press down firmly with the index finger which rests on the dull edge of the knife blade and points toward the tip.

Hold the fork in your left hand with the tines down. Rest your index finger on the spine of the inverted fork. Pierce and secure the meat with the fork.

Place the cutting edge of the knife slightly in front of the tines of the fork. Pull the knife toward you to cut the meat. Cut only one or two bites at a time.

A small wedge of a vegetable may be speared onto the tines of the fork along with the meat. Be careful not to stack food onto the fork.

The Dessert Course

The Difficult-to-Eat Dessert. Have you ever tried to eat food that went skidding off the plate when you put your fork or spoon to it? Frozen desserts often do that.

To avoid such a disaster, pick up the dessert fork and spoon that are above your plate or along either side of your plate. Hold the fork in your left hand, tines down.

Remember that a spoon should be held in your right hand. Eat with the spoon and use the inverted fork held in your left hand to secure a difficult dessert, such as a frozen one, while you spoon into it.

When you finish eating, place the fork and spoon in the "finished" position even if you used only one of them. When the meal is complete, your place should be clear of all silverware, except possibly a coffee spoon if coffee will be served at the table.

Other Desserts. Eat pie or cake with only the dessert fork. Eat ice cream or pudding with the dessert spoon. If you use only one utensil, leave the other one on the table while you eat.

Toasting Protocol

The host may make a toast before the appetizer or right before dessert. While remaining seated, he or she may make a toast before the meal to greet everyone. In anticipation of a toast, guests refrain from touching any of the beverages before the meal begins.

At the beginning of the dessert course, a host may propose a toast to honor one individual. For this closing gesture, the host stands. The honored guest remains seated. The guest may hold a glass, but should not engage in drinking to toast himself. Afterwards, the honored person may then rise and propose a toast in which he or she may participate. After the honored guest finishes, another guest may rise to propose a toast.

When a toast is proposed, it is acceptable to sip water from the water goblet, or you may raise an empty glass if you do not drink wine and there is no water glass.

The Meal Is Completed

The host signals that it is time to leave the table by placing his napkin to the left of his place. (His plate may or may not have been removed.) His napkin will rest loosely on the table with any unsightly smudges on the underside.

The guests then do the same with their napkins. Never refold a napkin. Never put a napkin in a used plate or glass.

Practice Makes Perfect

To acquire skill and confidence, you must practice your fine dining skills. Don't be frazzled at the sight of many forks or frightened by formalities.

Use as many of the new skills as possible every time you eat, no matter the place. Then you won't be overwhelmed and frustrated by details when you need to use the finer points of formal dining.

If you make a mistake or forget a rule, don't be discouraged. Relax and follow the lead of the host or that of others if no host is present. If you do everything slowly and carefully, you will look confident and avoid any embarrassing mishaps. Then when you get home, look up the rule. You will probably never forget that one again.

Dining in a Private Home

Dining rules are virtually the same whether we are in a restaurant or in someone's home, but knowing the difference is important, especially if we are entertained in our boss' home.

Our mistakes and blunders become magnified when we are in a smaller, more intimate environment. The boss is the chef or at the least, he or she is the overseer of all the preparations.

Perhaps no one was ever fired for dumping the gravy boat, but 99 executives out of 100 consider social skills as important as other business skills according to corporate research done by Randi Freidig, a business etiquette specialist in Seattle.[1] Here are some guidelines to help steer clear of job-jeopardizing embarrassment in a private home:

- Never arrive early, but be no more than ten minutes late.
- Never bring an uninvited guest unless you ask permission prior to the day of the dinner.
- If you are the guest of honor, take or send a hostess gift. Never take fresh-cut flowers with you. The hostess will be too busy to look for a vase. (You may have flowers delivered earlier.) If you don't see your hostess gift after you arrive, don't ask why it is not used or displayed.
- The rule that the guest of honor must leave first is no longer viable.
- All guests should stay thirty minutes to one hour after dinner unless they have informed the hostess beforehand that they must leave early. The best time for that is when she extends the invitation or as soon thereafter as possible.
- Don't go into the kitchen before, during, or after the meal unless the hostess invites. At formal dinners, guests usually do

not offer or assist in preparing the meal or in clearing the dishes.

- Greet the other guests and introduce yourself when appropriate; the host and/or hostess may be unable to do so. They likely will be occupied with answering the door and preparing dinner.

- Men should be prepared to escort a woman to the table if the host indicates partners before dinner. Usually husbands and wives are not seated together. The conversations at dinner flow better that way, and guests get to know one another.

- The host leads the way into the dining room with the female guest of honor (if there is one). The hostess and the male guest of honor (if there is one) go in last.

- A man assists the woman on his right with her chair (and also the woman on his left if she has no one to do it).

- After she sits, a woman should assist the man in pulling her chair forward to a comfortable position. She must grasp the sides of her chair and lift it slightly as she and the man together move the chair forward and under the table. More than one effort may be necessary.

- Wait to be told where to sit if there are no place cards. Usually either the host or hostess will ask guests to be seated. If you have no indicator of where to sit, you may take the chair nearest you.

- When seated, don't touch anything on the table.

- Watch the hostess for every cue, starting with the invocation and the lifting of the napkin, which usually are the first two movements to occur. Before beginning to eat each course you must also watch the hostess. Begin when she does. She will wait until everyone is served or instruct the guests to begin. Usually in a private home, grace is spoken before the hostess lifts her napkin. Simply watch closely.

- If a piece of flatware or a glass is missing from your place, quietly bring it to the hostess' attention. You may say, "I seem to be missing a dinner fork."
- Don't ask for seconds. If they are offered, you may accept, so long as others continue to eat.
- Don't ask for condiments or special items not on the table.
- Remember that seasoning your food heavily after the hostess prepared it is rude. Taste everything before salting.
- Don't ask what a dish is unless you compliment it first. Usually it is better not to ask questions about the food.
- Say thank you quietly each time you are served.
- At the table, never mention allergies or ailments regarding food or drink.
- Taste everything, if possible. Eat what you can. If you do not like something or cannot eat all the food, say, "I'm saving room for dessert." Do not wipe or scrape your plate clean. Diners are no longer required to leave some food on the plate, but it is not rude to do so.
- Always pick up your fork or spoon and at least pretend to be eating each course. To see a tablemate not eating makes other guests feel uncomfortable and causes them to wonder if they should be eating the dish before them.
- Use your napkin often, especially before sipping your beverage. Women should not blot their lips on the napkin.
- Dab your mouth. Don't swipe side to side. Replace the napkin in your lap with the folded edge toward your knees.
- Leave your napkin on your lap until the hostess places hers on the table, signaling that the meal is over.

- Never leave a dinner table temporarily unless it is absolutely necessary. If you must, place your napkin beside your plate, with any smudges hidden or in your chair. Never put a napkin in a dirty plate.
- You may make complimentary statements about the food occasionally, but not continuously.
- Remember that your spouse is a guest also. Treat him or her the same way you do other guests—without criticizing, arguing with, or interrupting.
- Never place used silverware back on the tablecloth. Prop the iced teaspoon on a plate or lay the bowl of it in another spoon to prevent staining the hostess's linens.
- Be prepared to serve yourself from a platter or large bowl if courses are presented to you by a server standing on your left. You may see two large serving pieces resting in the dish. If you remember that a spoon always goes in your right hand, you can easily lift a serving portion from the serving dish and onto your plate. Place the spoon under a piece of meat, for instance, and secure it with the tines of the fork. To do so, hold the inverted fork in your left hand with your index finger on the spine and the handle pointing into your palm.
- If soup, sauce, or gravy is in the dish, suspend your portion above the container long enough for the drips to subside. Transfer it quickly to your plate. Don't plop your serving onto your plate. Slide the spoon gently from beneath your portion.
- Replace the serving utensils in the dish in such a way that they will not slide down into the dish. Usually, placing them in an inverted position helps—bowl of the spoon and tines of the fork facing downward.

- Afternoon tea is served from 3:00 to 5:00 P.M. High tea is a light meal much like our supper. It is served later than afternoon tea.

ARRANGING LUNCH/DINNER
ENGAGEMENT WITH A CLIENT

In your file have a current list of places offering good service, pleasant atmosphere, good food, the right price, and a variety of food types.

Preparations

- Set the date (not too far in advance), time and place.
- Extend the invitation to client. Ask about food preferences.
- Choose the restaurant but not for glamour. Don't show off and sacrifice other amenities.
- Choose a restaurant you have eaten in prior to the date with the client.
- Call the restaurant maître d' and make the reservation.
- Give name, number in party, time of arrival, and any special arrangements such as table or food service.
- Make sure the room is large enough and quiet enough with convenient parking.
- Reserve a desirable table—not near the kitchen, restrooms, or telephones.
- Put everything in writing to the maître d' (if the event is large and especially important).

THE DAY OF THE DINING MEETING

- Confirm the time and location with the client the day before.
- Arrive ten minutes early. Wait in the foyer for the client.
- After arrival of first guest, wait ten minutes then ask maître d' to seat you. Wait another ten minutes for any remaining guest(s) to arrive before ordering.
- Always place the client(s) in the best seat(s).
- Instruct your guest to order whatever he/she likes (if your budget will allow).
- Discuss business only after you have ordered and chatted a few minutes.
- Tip the maître d' or captain five dollars in a handshake as you leave.

TABLE MANNERS MATTER

- Place no elbows on the table, unless all dishes are removed following the meal.
- Chew with your mouth closed.
- Hold the silverware correctly.
- Cut one bite of meat at a time.
- Pass food to your right.
- Serve food from the left of the diner and remove the soiled plate from the right.
- Serve beverages from the right of the diner.
- Pass both the salt and pepper.
- Break bread in half or pinch one bite at a time. Never take a big chomp out of food.
- Keep feet flat on the floor and under the table.
- Sit up straight in your chair.
- Modify your voice so that only your tablemates can hear you.
- Excuse yourself to people on each side of you if you must leave the table.
- Refuse food only if you must by saying, "No, thank you."
- Pass the butter dish with the butter knife on the dish.
- Stir iced tea quietly. Cover your hand to squeeze the lemon over the glass.
- Say, "Please pass the. . . ."
- Watch to see that all condiments near you are passed around the table.
- Unfold the restaurant napkin halfway. Place the fold toward your knees.
- Place your napkin, gently crumpled, to the left of your place setting when the meal is finished. When excusing yourself momentarily, place your napkin beside the plate or in your chair.

- Eat at a moderate speed. Don't make others wait for you to finish.
- Place used silverware on a plate, not on the tablecloth (even during a course).
- Watch the hostess in a home for beginnings and endings and which flatware to use.
- Eat quietly, making no noise with your mouth or silverware.
- Remove seeds, pits, gristle, etc. from your mouth with the utensil you used to put it in your mouth. Do not use your napkin, because the discarded particle could get on your clothes or could be dropped to the floor. Small bones may be removed with one's thumb and forefinger (for safety).
- Hold cold beverages by supporting the bowl of the glass from underneath, holding the bowl with your thumb and fingers on the stem.
- Refuse a beverage by simply saying, "No, thank you." Do not invert the cup or glass.
- Refuse alcohol by simply saying, "No, thank you." No explanation is necessary.

WORKING WITH A CATERER

The boss says, "Set up a company dinner and submit the plans to me." It may be an office party or a working luncheon in the boardroom. You are expected to know how to do it. Don't panic. Here is a plan:

1. Get Organized
   - Set the date and time, and make out the guest list.
   - Choose the location for the dinner based on the date, size, type of function, budget, and suitable decor.
   - Require that all bids and plans by the caterer (and all suppliers) be made in writing.

2. Select the Caterer
   - Choose a caterer by using the word of mouth or networking method.
   - Meet with a prospective caterer face-to-face, if possible, and get an estimate. Offer to write a letter of recommendation if all goes well.
   - Establish the method of payment (with all suppliers) and inquire about any necessary deposit, the cancellation policy, and the inclement weather policy.
   - Ask about the temperature and the visual presentation of the food. Provide variety in the menu to include some low-fat meat.
   - Discuss the menu and condiments.
   - Once the right choice of caterer is made, you may give the caterer every detail and then leave it to him or her. Incessant nagging can destroy efficiency.
   - Decide on the table arrangement. Make it conducive to the meeting after the meal and convenient to accommodate latecomers.
   - Decide on how the table will be set. Will the flatware, courses, and beverages be on the table when guests arrive or served later?
   - If paper plates are used, they must be of substantial weight.

- The servers must have spotless uniforms, clean and pressed. Their grooming (hair, nails, etc.) must be impeccable. Their attitude should be pleasant and helpful.

- Be prepared to tip the head waiter twenty dollars and the waiters ten dollars unless other arrangements have been made with the caterer and/or restaurant.

3. Choose and Send the Invitations

   - The invitations should show the date, social hour, dining time, location, attire, purpose of function, and the name of the host (person or company). See correspondence chapter for more on invitations.

4. Engage a Florist

   - Choose the florist and approve the centerpiece. It should be below eye level. You don't want it to obstruct the guests' view across the table.

5. Write a Plan B

   - Discuss with the caterer some "what ifs," such as if there is not enough food or the servers don't arrive on time.

6. Serve as Host/Hostess

   As host/hostess, you will be responsible for seeing that guests have what they need.

   - Keep the noise level of any food helpers down.

   - Don't spend too much time with one guest.

   - Be alert and perceptive to needs.

   - Be discreet.

   - Don't complain or apologize profusely if something goes wrong.

7. Follow Up

   - If the room is in a private home or club and not in a public restaurant, remain after the guests leave to see that the room is cleaned. The next day you don't want someone to ask indignantly, "Who used this room last?"

- Send a thank-you letter to each supplier who provided good service. Include the promised recommendation (signed by your boss, if possible).

- Keep a good record of past menus and guest lists if you plan meals on a regular basis for your company where many of the same people attend.

What to Do When Professionally Entertained

- Answer all invitations as quickly as possible. Your secretary may respond, but if you must cancel with regrets, only you should do that.

- Inquire about any unclear information in the invitation. Your secretary can do that. There may be doubt about dress or location or such.

- Know the names of your host and hostess and the company responsible for the party or dinner. Prepare your spouse with the same information.

- Get a list of attendees, if possible, so you and your spouse will appear informed.

- Prepare for conversation by reading headlines, watching TV news, etc.

- Take the invitation with you in the car.

- Arrive on time—never early and never later than ten minutes.

- Send flowers to the hostess prior to the evening if you are the guest of honor.

- Feel free to have a nonalcoholic drink or no drink at all. Make no explanation.

- Introduce yourself and your spouse to other guests.

- Wait to be told where to sit. Wait until all guests are standing behind their chairs before being seated. The man seats the lady to his right and any other lady if he sees a need. The hostess signals when and where to sit.

- Make conversation with the person to your right and to your left at the table.

- Eat one serving unless hostess offers more. If seconds are offered, you may accept or say, "No, thank you."

- Avoid all argumentative topics such as politics and religion.

- Avoid all references to dieting and calories.

- Eat at the same pace as other diners.

- Place your napkin on the table beside your plate and rise after the hostess signals the meal is over by placing her napkin beside her plate and rising.

- Know when to leave. When professionally entertained, stay at least thirty minutes after the meal.

- Say, "I had a great time," or "Thank you for inviting me," or a similar adieu, but *never say* "I enjoyed myself."

- Say your goodbyes before putting on your coat.

- Write a thank-you note. If the dinner/party was in the host/hostess's home, the husband writes to the host at his office graciously mentioning the hostess. The wife writes a note to the hostess mentioning the host. Her note is mailed to the home if it was a business/social evening in the home. Heavy-weight notepaper is best.

CHAPTER 9

Business/Social Conversation

The best way to persuade others is with our ears.

Rusk

What Is Your EQ? Business Small Talk

1. Do you know how and when to begin a conversation with someone you don't know?

2. What are open-ended questions, and how are they useful?

3. Do you know the protocol for carrying on a conversation with your boss?

4. Do you know how to deal politely with another's nosy questions?

5. Do you know how to escape an interminable talker without being offensive?

The social side of business often forces us to make small talk with people we hardly know. If we find it difficult to talk about trivial or nonbusiness matters, we usually dread going to business/social events.

Of course, some individuals never lack for something to say. Those people sometimes get into trouble by saying the wrong thing at the wrong time.

In Business, Small Talk Must Be Smart Talk

Without a little chitchat we have no common ground for establishing a rapport with someone. We can't carry on a meaningful conversation. Most of us have trouble getting started, knowing what topic to bring up, fearing we will say the wrong thing in our "politically correct" society.

Polite conversation, no matter the setting, is somewhat like playing ball. One individual throws out a topic and the other person catches it and returns a volley. At least that is the way it should be, but all of us have been caught in small-talk traps where no one says anything and the chill of silence hangs heavy in the room. What to do next?

Here are some guidelines for you to adapt to your personality and to the setting in which you find yourself. The occasion may be formal or informal. You may be sitting or standing with one person next to you, or you may be in a group of people at work or at a social gathering.

Find Common Ground

Don't worry about being clever or even original. Venture out with a statement to find something you have in common with the other person. If you are at a buffet dinner, standing around trying to balance a plate and a cup or glass, mention the food or a particular dish you find tasty: "Did you get some of this dip? I think it's delicious. Do you happen to know what it is called?" Your primary purpose is to convey warmth and interest in someone. Look in the person's face and gesture toward the dip. Don't stare at the food on your plate and mutter your question.

What you do after asking your question is extremely important. Listen carefully to your partner's answer. If you are lucky, you will hear something besides yes or no. The person will add some tidbit to his or her answer, and you will have a springboard for something else to talk about. Breaking the ice, as the saying goes, is the first hurdle to overcome.

Getting Started

If you are even slightly acquainted with the individual, bring up the name of a mutual friend: "The last time I saw you, you were with Joe. Have you seen him lately?"

If Joe was an old boyfriend and she says, "No, Joe and I broke up long ago. We barely speak these days," you say, "Oh," then swallow your momentary embarrassment and move on to another subject. Don't be discouraged. Similar faux pas happen to all of us. A faux pas of mine was to ask how someone's mother was doing, and I was reminded that she had died. (I had forgotten.) I felt awful.

In making small talk, simply remember to be positive and complimentary about your host, the occasion, and the surroundings. After you establish a rapport with your partner in conversation, you can consider expressing a mild negative if you worry about sounding like a naïve Pollyanna: "You know, I had such a late lunch with a client today that I'm really not hungry. I usually eat dinner much later." Be careful because saying that when the host might overhear is rude.

The weather is an awful topic to use to begin a conversation, and yet it is one of the most effective. It's boring, but safe. I suggest that rather than mentioning only the present state of the weather, say something about how it has helped or hindered your lifestyle lately. For instance, if you are at a dinner party, say, "I see that we all made it here on time despite this heavy rainstorm. Did you have far to come?"

If you can think of nothing to say, compliment some aspect of the other person's appearance. "I like your tie. Matching ties to suits has always been difficult for me." Your partner might say, "Thank you. I picked this up last summer when we were on vacation in New England." He or she has brought up the subjects of travel, vacations, and a specific area of the country. You have three new subjects to pursue.

To a woman you can say, "I like your briefcase." She may say, "Thank you. My son and daughter-in-law gave it to me." You have learned she has a married child. You can ask if they live nearby or mention that you, too, have a grown son.

Conversing with a Company Superior

Perhaps you are flying with your boss to a meeting across the country. Let your employer take the lead in deciding what you will discuss. If he or she brings up business, the employee should show that his or her mind is on business. For instance, the employee may mention some bit of news about the competition: "I'm told that Affiliated Products is trying to buy out Associated Materials." Such a statement is neither negative, pessimistic, nor boring. You have left the discussion open for the boss to decide where to take it. He can talk about the negative or the positive of how that buyout might affect your business. You will then have a clue about the tone to use in further discussions.

When the Boss Is Silent

The junior employee should permit the senior person to choose the subject of conversation or choose not to converse at all. Watch for cues.

- If the employer does not talk, he or she may be tired, may need to think something through, or may prefer to read or work.
- If the senior person answers questions perfunctorily, he is probably not in the mood for conversation.
- After a time, the senior executive may lay down what he is reading or working on and ask the younger person a question.
- If the senior wants to continue the dialogue, he or she will ask other questions or make comments indicating a readiness to talk.

- If the boss wants to engage in light conversation unrelated to business, the employee should be prepared with some amusing stories—told in good taste of course.
- The boss may prefer to tell his or her own stories without listening to the employee's. In business, the junior employee always "yields the floor."

Conversational Dilemmas

Sometimes the subject we are discussing becomes boring. We feel trapped. We know that switching topics of conversation too quickly can be rude, especially when the other person brought up the topic. Here are some suggestions.

Conversation Detours

Provide a springboard. After a brief silence, bring up a topic that was mentioned earlier. For instance: "You mentioned earlier that you will be spending the summer in Alaska. How delightful that sounds. I'd like to hear about your plans."

Redirect. Another way to change the subject is to change directions on a positive note. Make a complimentary remark about the current topic and then shift to another one: "You have really kept up with the new age of technology. I wish I could say the same. Now, tell me how you and Margaret, whom I have known for years, got acquainted."

Graceful Escapes

Conversing with the same person sometimes keeps going long after we have lost interest in the person or the topic. How do we gracefully escape? Here are some tips:

- Switch your signals. Stop responding with nods of agreement or saying "uh-huh" or "Is that right?" or "How interesting."

- Use red-light signals. Move back a step. Look away occasionally. Don't talk unless you are asked a direct question. Soon the silence that follows will give you a way out.
- Say something positive, such as, "It was good to talk to you. You have enlightened me on . . ." State what you need to do. "I must say hello to John. He's from out-of-town, and I'm afraid I'll miss his short visit." Start moving away and say, "It was so nice to meet you. I hope we can visit again."

Dealing with Nosy, Personal Questions

People can ask us all sorts of questions that are none of their business. Observing proper etiquette does not force us to answer any of them directly, but we are required to respond with tact and grace. To retort with an angry, "That's none of your business" may be justified and may even make us feel better momentarily, but saying that means we are as brash as they. Here are some appropriate tactics.

Avoid answering directly. You know immediately when someone is fishing for some juicy tidbit about your personal life. Avoid giving them what they want to hear. Say, "I know that many people today feel comfortable talking about the reason for their divorce, but I guess I'm somewhat old-fashioned. That part of my life is behind me." Then bring up a subject more comfortable for you: "Did you get to see my new grandson on baby dedication Sunday at church a few weeks ago?"

Use humor. When people try to uncover the name of your favorite baby-sitter so they can engage her ahead of you, say, "Oh, I can't tell you all my secrets."

Be vague. When someone poses a question to learn how much you get paid, rephrase their question with what they really want you to say, "How much money do I make? Oh, I get by," or say, "Not as much as I should, I assure you."

When someone tries to learn your age, they usually ask questions such as, "What year did you get married? (or finish school)," say, "Oh, we married in—; I was a child bride of course."

Another way to avoid answering directly is to say, "I can't believe you would really be interested in all the boring details," or, "We really don't have time here to go into all that."

Turn the tables. Someone asks you if you used drugs in college. Respond with, "Why don't you tell me about your college days first. They must be far more interesting than mine."

Annoying Interruptions

If we often get cut off in the middle of telling our story, we may be talking too long. If so, we should wrap up our story quickly. On the other hand, we may be sending some wrong signals.

Conversational cues that may help avoid being interrupted include:

1. Don't pause too long or your listeners will assume you are finished.
2. Don't drop the pitch of your voice until you completely finish your comment or story.
3. Use a hand signal. Raise your index finger to signal "wait" and keep on talking. The others in the group probably resent, as much as you do, those people who interrupt out of rudeness or selfishness.
4. Talk privately. If this happens often with the same person, talk to him or her before the next event and say, "Before we go to this meeting (or party) I need to discuss something with you. Perhaps, without realizing it, you get carried away and interrupt me every time I get the floor to speak."

Proxemics

You, no doubt, know people who stand so close to you that to see them you must look through the bifocals of your glasses. I don't know if they are nearsighted, hearing impaired, or what, but their closeness makes us feel very uncomfortable.

I had a professor in college who clanked his false teeth and often showered the front-row students as he lectured; hence, no one wanted to sit up front. Everyone moved to a back row.

The Rule of Proximity

A familiar term explaining proximity today is "our private space," meaning the nearness of two people. Not everyone's space is the same distance, but we should usually stand about an arm's length away from the person. If you see the other person lean backward slightly or even step backward, you know you are standing or sitting too closely for their comfort.

Establishing Your Private Space

Most of us have an intuitive sense of how far apart we like to sit or stand from others. If chairs are set up, we may slide ours away slightly from the one next to it before we sit. If possible, we may choose a seat with some empty space on one side or both.

When a woman gets too close, we may see the tiny facial hairs over her lip. If the intruder is a man, we may see the shave line on his face or the pores in his nose. If you would just as soon not get that close to someone, you will need to reestablish your private space.

First, take a step backward, hoping he or she will not follow. When such a minor adjustment in position fails and the invader is again in your face, inch your way over so that a piece of furniture such as a table or a chair is between you.

Second, if you encounter this space invader often (perhaps in your office) and you know that he or she is on the way to your office, arrange two chairs three feet apart. Point to one of the chairs and say, "Please have a seat."

Finally, if subtle efforts fail, you may have to say, "I enjoy talking to you, but I feel more comfortable with a little more distance between me and the person I talk to—whoever it is. I know you won't mind."

Suggestions for Successful Conversations

General Suggestions

- When we ask someone, "How are you?" we should listen attentively for the answer before rushing into what we want to say. We should use the word "you" more than "I."
- In chitchat situations, be brief. This is not the time for long answers. We must remember we are playing conversational pitch as with a ball. Don't hold the ball too long. Thirty seconds is long enough to hold the floor in most instances. Talking for a minute is a speech.
- Remember to stand or sit at least eighteen inches away.
- Ask open-ended questions. Any question that requires more than a yes or no answer is an open-ended question. "Tell me about your vacation" is better than "Have you taken a vacation this year?"
- Be sincere (without pretense or deceit). People recognize a phony.

- Be brief in your answers, however saying only yes or no is too brief.
- Feel confident that you will have something to contribute. Everyone has some experience to share.
- Turn self-consciousness into self-confidence by concentrating on the other person and not on what you are going to say next. People sense it when you are not "tuned in" to them.
- Be prepared to share something about yourself. If you never volunteer any information, you drop the ball. People trust us more when we expose a *little* of our thoughts and feelings.
- Be informed about the news of the day by print media or television. You want to respond to questions intelligently but not tell all you know about the subject. Remember that "knowledge should be like a fine gold watch. Keep it in your pocket unless someone asks the time."
- Be familiar with the latest movies and books whether or not you see or read them.
- Keep the mood light by interjecting a little humor where and when it is appropriate. People like us better when we joke about our own mistakes or inadequacies.
- Don't tell or laugh at ethnic jokes or off-color stories.
- Don't blast away at your conversation partner with a barrage of questions. Integrate questions with positive statements.
- Don't interrupt. Don't finish someone else's thought, even if you are positive you know the word he or she is struggling to remember.
- Don't ask someone to relate a particular story and then take over the telling of it. Spouses are tempted to do that because they have heard each other's stories so many times.

- Don't interrupt someone's story to correct the facts you are sure were misstated. It really does not matter whether the event happened last June or last July.
- Don't echo what someone says by repeating a word or two after each thought.
- Don't correct another's grammar or pronunciation of words.
- Don't be known as the person who can talk about nothing but work.
- Don't bear your soul to an acquaintance.
- Don't be a complainer. People have their own troubles.
- Don't show pictures of your children or grandchildren unless people ask to see them.
- Don't bring up the subject of salaries or the pay scale. About the only safe topic concerning money is the cost of living.
- Don't mention labor unions if both labor and management personnel are present.
- Don't bring up argumentative subjects such as politics or religion. You may mention the church you attend, but don't bring up doctrinal beliefs that might create an argument or heated discussion.
- Don't tell anything that will make another person look bad.
- Laugh with the group if someone tells something humorous about you, as long as it is in good taste.
- Don't blurt out, "What do you do for a living?" It is better to say, "I'm in sales. What do you do?" Even though you are seeking common ground for conversation, you may appear to be interested only in how much money they make. If you offer some information about your job first, you appear less intrusive.

- Don't answer every question with a simple yes or no. For instance, if someone asks, "Did you ever go on a cruise?" don't just say, "No." Say something like, "No, but my wife and I have talked about it. We just never seem to get around to it."
- Don't be embarrassed when you must say no. Not everyone's interests are the same. Not everyone has the same adventurous spirit or the same opportunities.
- Don't make the other person feel bad that they don't have the same interests you have. If you keep trying, you will discover something the two of you have in common to talk about.

Selective Honesty

Whether in the office, with a client, or in a social setting, choose your words carefully. Selective honesty shows professional style.

Total honesty can be carelessness masquerading as freedom of speech, which then becomes self-indulgent assertiveness. For instance, we hear statements such as "You want to know what I really think, don't you?" or "You want me to be perfectly honest, don't you?"

Honesty can be an excuse for an unmannerly comment or a way to vent one's true feelings: "I think you must be putting on weight," or "My therapist told me to get my anger out and that is why I yelled at you." However, as Jill Robinson, in *House and Garden* magazine said, some of us "would very much like to see some feelings covered up."[1]

What some people consider "being direct," and therefore more honest, is actually hurtful to others. Selective honesty does not mean we have to lie. Without making a direct, unkind response, we can always find something nice to say about a disaster. Take, for example, a bad haircut: "Your new, short haircut must be cooler in this hot summer we are having." It is seldom that we should tell everything we know or feel.

A Kind Critique

When you do find it necessary to correct another person, you might say, "There seems to be a discrepancy here," instead of "You made a mistake," or "You're wrong."

While we may have more experience than someone else, we should permit the other person to find his or her own errors. When we begin a comment with an accusatory, critical, tactless, or harsh tone, such as "In my opinion," or "You should not have," we immediately put the other person on the defensive. We must give him or her a chance to respond or contribute to the solution.

When offering a suggestion, begin with "Could we try," or "What do you think of."

While attempting to set the situation right, the goal is to defuse tension because tension cuts down on efficiency and creativity.

Avoid Offensive Language

In 1991, the National Institute of Business Management did not think it necessary to even address the issue of offensive language. Yet today cursing and swearing, even talk of bodily functions, are a problem everywhere. Using language that offends is a serious breach of business or social etiquette. According to a 1995 publication issued by the institute, "Foul language is inappropriate."[2]

Because people break these rules all the time, it is important to know how to deal with offensive language, off-color jokes, gossip, and comments with sexual overtones.

When faced with such language, we can show our discomfort by saying something like, "Let's get down to business. We have a lot of work yet to do."[3]

Ethnic or racial slurs against individuals or groups can get your paycheck reduced or even get you fired. A New York journalist was suspended for two weeks without pay for responding to a criticism of one of his columns as "sexist" with an ethnic slur.

Topics for Conversation

Use the guidelines above and some of the following topics to help you engage in chitchat without "putting your foot in your mouth." You might want to look over this list before leaving for an event. Your small talk can be smart talk.

Suggested Topics

In addition to previously suggested topics, any of the following subjects are acceptable:

- place of origin
- hobbies
- travel
- schools attended
- places you have lived
- previous occupations
- sports
- arts and entertainment
- the next Olympics
- health clubs
- trends in business
- pets
- space travel
- gourmet cooking
- current museum offerings

- how two spouses met
- community activities
- the Internet
- new technology
- books
- movies
- grandchildren (if everyone present has them)
- family genealogy (if someone has an interesting or unusual last name, you can ask if they have traced their lineage, but don't pry into their history. It may be embarrassing.)

Topics to Avoid

It is always a good idea to avoid the following topics:
- personal medical status or history (yours or someone else's)
- dieting
- weight
- personal finances
- gory subjects
- politics
- any argumentative subject

Inappropriate Questions to Ask

Don't ask
- if a rumor is true
- how much someone weighs
- what size dress, suit, or shoe someone wears
- if the person has dyed or bleached his or her hair
- someone's age if they are obviously over thirty
- the price someone paid for a house or car
- the terms of someone's divorce settlement
- why someone is bald or obviously losing hair
- if the person has had cosmetic surgery
- about the state of a person's marriage
- about anyone's sex life

Developing People Skills

To be successful with people, we need to keep some succinct points in mind. First, *concentrate on the other person*. Most of us think about ourselves too much—what we are going to say and do. Although it takes practice, focusing on the needs of others is far more satisfying, even more fun.

Get People to Talk About Themselves.

If you know the person well enough you can ask questions such as
- "How is your family, John?"
- "How far along in school is your daughter now?"
- "Did you enjoy your trip (vacation, meal, weekend)?"
- "What do you think of this place (event, decor, occasion)?"
- "How long have you been with the company?"

Be Agreeable

- Don't argue, even if you are right.
- Use a quiet, controlled voice to defuse your tension or someone's anger.
- Say at least one kind thing to at least three people daily.

Be a Good Listener

- Look at the person with focus, but don't stare blankly.
- Lean forward slightly toward the speaker or at least keep your body squarely facing the individual.
- Ask questions at the appropriate time.
- Don't interrupt or change the subject abruptly.
- Listen by making mental notes of key words spoken so you can respond intelligently. With a few of those words you can ask a question or use them to make a comment later.
- Listen carefully to everything the individual says before forming definite opinions.
- Don't assume facts not stated or prejudge his or her intentions.

Make a Good and Lasting Impression

- Be sincere (without pretense). Don't flatter manipulatively. Flattery is exaggerated praise that may not be true. Comment on the individual's accomplishments instead.

- Show enthusiasm. It's contagious.
- Don't try to inflate your own image by running down someone else.
- Don't criticize. Disparaging remarks and criticism only make the speaker look foolish and insecure.

Call people by name often. Say, "Thank you, Ms. Smith," rather than a simple "Thank you."

Specific People Skills for Business Settings

In order to succeed in business we must satisfy our customers and clients. This involves dealing with different types of individuals as we assess their needs and do our best to meet these needs pleasantly and competently.

The Angry or "Know-It-All" Customer

- Remain calm and polite.
- Agree when possible.
- Avoid overexplaining your position by repetition and/or talking too long.
- Be noticeably silent while the other person is talking.
- Don't argue.
- Remember, you may not be the real target or the real cause of the other's anger.

The Impatient Customer or Employee

- Politely explain policy, such as "taking a number."
- Maintain a demeanor of confidence, but not arrogance.
- Reassure the customer of service as soon as possible.

"People spend approximately 70 percent of their time communicating; listening accounts for 45 percent of this time."[4]

The Shy Customer

- Remain patient and be sympathetic.
- Ask questions to establish customer's needs.
- Attempt to clear up any confusion.

The Customer That Gets Too Personal

- Remain businesslike and calm.
- Ignore or pretend not to hear innuendos.
- Don't threaten or become defensive.
- Avoid eye contact.
- Move on to the next customer as soon as possible.

Of course, there are situations when the remarks become too personal and must be reported (see "Sexual Harrassment" in chapter 2).

Dealing with Customer Complaints

Good manners means letting others tell you what you already know.

"It's a matter of survival. Customers are demanding quality service." U.S. Chamber of Commerce, *Nation's Business.*

When you see a customer approaching you with a complaining look on his or her face, it is not time to get defensive. You do, however, want to be prepared. Here are some suggestions for dealing with the complaining customer as you take steps to solve his or her problem.

Listen to the Customer. The customer's needs must be met. It is up to us to determine the need. It may be that the customer simply needs to have his say in the matter.

Speaking is often associated with authority, while listening may be falsely perceived as a sign of subservience. It takes a sense of being in control when we can truly listen to an irate or irrational speaker.

- Continue to smile, but do not grin. Grins appear sarcastic.
- Think of yourself as calm and confident. It will show.
- Use a quiet, controlled voice.
- Accept the customer's complaint as stated.
- Be empathetic (listen for understanding, not simply agreement or disagreement): "I can appreciate your being upset. Let me see what I can do to help."
- Don't interrupt.
- Ask questions to show you care. Be sure to utilize the "stop rule"—Ask a question, then stop and listen for the answer.
- Write down pertinent facts and claims.
- If appropriate, admit company or personal responsibility.
- Offer a solution according to company policy if you are authorized to do so.
- If all the above fails, assure the customer you will search for a solution. If possible, give a few details about steps you will take to find one.

Take Steps to Solve the Problem

- Determine the problem and the cause.
- Don't assume that all the customer's information is fact. Do your own research.

Present the Solution

- Go over the problem and your suggested solution with the customer.
- Seek the customer's agreement to the solution.

Utilizing "Tactful Talk"

Proper social etiquette deems that some things are better left unsaid. The same is true in business. For example, when someone asks a question to which we do not know the answer, we may be tempted to simply say, "I don't know"; however, in business we are paid to know or to find out. We need to respond honestly but in a way that maintains the customers good will.

> "Be kind. Everyone you meet is fighting a hard battle." *T. H. Thompson*

The following responses are six examples of things *not* to say along with their tactful alternatives.

1. *"I don't know."*

A better way to answer would be, "I'll find out and get back to you as soon as possible. Can I reach you at this number?" Follow up quickly.

2. *"We can't do that."*

Say something such as, "That is a difficult one. Let me find out what we can do about that." Don't remind the customer of what you can't do. Repeating negatives won't help.

If you find you really are unable to help, calmly explain the company policy or procedures. If possible, ask the customer what they would like you to do. Satisfying the customer is often easier than we fear.

3. *"You will have to. . . ."*

Customers do not have to do anything; they can take their business elsewhere. Say, "Here is how we can help with that" or "I will have the person in charge of that contact you. Is this the correct telephone number?" Follow up.

4. *"Hang on, I'll be right back."*

It is better to say, "It may take a minute or two. Can you hold?" Wait for an answer.

5. *"No."*

The word "No" used alone is very negative. It conveys total rejection. We can usually turn any answer into a positive one, such as, "We can . . . at no charge (or for a minimal fee)."

6. *"That's not my job."*

Our job description usually does not matter to the customer. We can say, "Come with me and we will find someone who is in charge of that."

> "Your test as a listener comes when you measure what you learn from others."[5]

CHAPTER 10

Business Correspondence

The deepest principle in human nature
is the need to be appreciated.
William James

What Is Your EQ? Business Correspondence

1. What is the only appropriate title in a signature?
2. What are the two most appropriate phrases for a good "closing" in business letters?
3. Should copies be signed?
4. What is the proper way to fold a business letter and insert it into the envelope?
5. Is it appropriate to make a personal reference in a business letter?

Remember the old question about the tree falling in the forest? If no one is there to hear it crash, does it make a sound? We could ask a similar question about business correspondence. Does sending a letter, facsimile, or E-mail message mean we are communicating? It is only when the recipient understands and acts that we know our correspondence achieved results.

Technology is changing the way we do business faster than ever in history. We have facsimile machines, modems, interactive laser disks, mail with a voice, and computers with megahertz to speed our transmissions and responses within the office and literally across the world.

Yet, what good are all the bells and whistles if we are not sending clear, concise, direct communiqués? Proper etiquette will always be necessary because we have not yet replaced the need for personal communication.

With new technology arriving daily, most of us have questions about the new rules. This chapter is not Office Machines 101, but it will offer some answers. As communicating electronically becomes more complicated, diverse, impersonal, dangerous, and less private, business protocol must keep pace. Otherwise we create misconceptions, leave false impressions, make bad impressions, hurt feelings, and bungle business deals.

Knowing the rules gives us confidence—an antidote to the overdose of office equipment surrounding us in the business world.

The Business Letter

Of all the forms of communication with individuals outside our company, the business letter is the most formal. It usually contains important information, such as a proposal, a response to a proposal, or the confirmation of a transaction.

Informal business letters deal with more personal matters than business alone. They perform an efficient function and indirectly enhance the image of the letter writer, whether the sender is a farmer, a florist, or an investment banker. These letters should follow the same structure as the formal letter, but the content usually reflects a more heartfelt message, such as a welcome to the business community with an offer of assistance, or a letter of congratulations for some achievement.

In a society dominated by computers, business letters must be succinct and written in the proper format. The format is the stage on which we launch our message.

Business letters should be typed, error free, on a company letterhead. They make a permanent record. Each letter written on business stationery is a personal emissary from one office to another. The paper stock, the letterhead on the company stationery, the way we set up a letter, and what we say all leave an impression about us and the business we represent.

Parts of a Business Letter

The essential elements of a business letter are the letterhead, date, inside address, salutation, body, and the closing.

The Letterhead. The letterhead should include: the company name, logo (if one exists), address, phone number, and fax number. If your corporate letterhead is personalized, your name with your title aligned below it should appear beneath and to the right of the company's name. Some firms choose to place the address, telephone number, and fax number at the bottom of the paper.

The quality of the paper is important. It should be a high-quality cotton-fiber paper that will take engraving or thermography.

A company letterhead should not be used for (1) controversial letters to the media; (2) personal matters, such as a lawsuit in which the company is not involved; or (3) purely personal matters, such as a love letter.

If you do not have "second sheets" for your letterheads, use another piece of letterhead with the proper number centered at the top.

You may use stationery with an old address or telephone number for about one month while new stationery is being printed. Cross out the old information and write the new.

The Date. The date should be (1) centered beneath the letterhead, (2) placed beneath the letterhead in the upper right-hand corner, or (3) flush with the left margin. Caveat: The date must always be aligned with the signature.

The Inside Address. The inside address should be four lines below the date. Always use a title in the inside address such as The Honorable Melinda Mays (title comes before). For attorneys you may abbreviate "Esquire" following the name such as Mark Ulmstead, Esq. Use no title such as "Mr." before Mark if "Esquire" is used.

"Jr." is not considered a title, but a part of the name. Therefore, you will use a title such as "Mr." before the name such as Mr. John Pate, Jr. When the senior Mr. Pate dies, the "Jr." designation is no longer necessary.

Use a proper title before or after the name on an envelope unless the addressee is a young man (see "Addressing Envelopes" on page 117). Never address a letter to Alice Smith without a title before or after the name. It should be (1) Ms. (or Dr.) Alice Smith, (2) Mrs. Allen Smith, or (3) Alice Smith, Executive Manager.

The Salutation. The salutation is placed two lines below the inside address. In a business letter, use a colon after the salutation; in a hand-written note, use a comma. "Dear" followed by the person's first name should only be used if you are already well acquainted and on a first name basis. Never use a first name unless you have been asked to do so or you have met the individual and feel comfortable using the first name.

Designations such as "Esq.," "Jr.," and "Honorable" are not included with a name in the salutation. However, a title such as "Mr.," "Mrs.," or "Dr." is usually used before the name.

The Body. The body of the letter begins one line below the salutation. Write in a conversational way, and don't use big words to impress. Short sentences of ten to twelve words often make stronger points. Be direct, concise, and positive. Avoid sounding pompous. Don't write repetitively to fill space.

To get to the point of the letter quickly, visualize the person to whom you are writing. List what you want to say before beginning to write. Make sure that the first paragraph, if not the first line, states the purpose of the letter. Finding the point should not become a scavenger hunt.

Two good beginnings are "Thank you for accepting my telephone call this afternoon," or "It was a pleasure to meet you this morning." Using "I" too much is considered bad form. Start with "You," or "Thank you," or even "It."

In an informal business letter, you may include a word or two of personal wishes in either the first or last paragraph. You may choose to pen a personal (not intimate) note at the bottom of the letter if no other eyes will see it. You may choose to enclose a separate piece of paper with the more private information (the recipient may need to circulate the formal letter). Use only black or navy blue ink.

When should one make a personal reference in a business note or letter? If you have met a member of an individual's family, it is good to send your regards to them if you know they remain associated with the individual you are writing. For instance, you may not know if two people remain married. If you are unsure, don't mention the spouse by name.

Avoid mentioning a personal occurrence in someone's life unless the person has told you or knows that you know the news, such as a divorce or an illness in the family.

If an individual has discussed a personal project he or she has undertaken, it is good to express good wishes about the progress.

After completing the letter, read it aloud. Check the first two paragraphs: Do they say anything of substance? If not, delete or reword them.

Because communication must be understood to be acted upon, ask these questions: Is my phrasing clear in meaning? Are the reader's needs addressed? Is the overall tone pleasant? Will the letter or note achieve the results I want?

Do not seal the letter or note immediately. Lay it aside and read it again before sealing. In some circumstances, you may want to ask someone to read it for clarity before you mail it.

The Closing. The closing is typed two lines below the body. Use "Sincerely" or "Sincerely yours."

The Signature. The signature line is dropped four lines below the closing to provide room for the handwritten signature. Type your first and last names. Remember to sign your name. Failure to sign a letter is not uncommon, but it is a sign of carelessness.

Titles before a name are not used in the signature block. A married woman signs "Katrina Ryan." When her social name should be revealed to the recipient, she signs "Katrina Ryan" and beneath that line, she puts "Mrs. Keith Ryan" in parentheses.

In social correspondence, a gentleman signs only his name: Wendell Holmes, not Dr. Wendell Holmes or Wendell Holmes, Ph.D.

The exception—if the reader does not know the signer and the signer's first name can be either male or female, the signer may put "Mr.," "Ms.," or "Mrs." in parentheses before the name such as (Mr.) Kiley Abel.

Copies. When making copies of the letter, place "c:" one line below the signature block. Sign only the original letter and keep an unsigned copy in your files. Place a check mark beside the typed-in name of each recipient's courtesy copy.

Folding the Business Letter

The following steps indicate the proper way to fold a standard 8 ½" X 11" business letter:

1. With the first page of the letter facing you, fold the lower edge of the letter upward approximately two-thirds from the bottom (leaving one-third at the top).

2. Fold the top edge down and over your previous work to the fold which you created.

3. The paper is now divided into thirds. Hold the envelope by the bottom edge in your left hand with the flap open to face you. Insert the folded letter with your right hand so that when it is removed from the envelope, the letter can be opened facing the reader. (The first fold and the top edge of the letter—which now meets that fold—will enter the envelope first.)

For a square or unfolded card or foldover note, insert it right-side-up into the envelope. Hold the envelope the same way you did for the letter. The message should face the reader when the recipient pulls the item from the envelope.

Notes

Occasions for sending a note, even in business, include but are not limited to congratulations, condolences, goodbyes, bon voyages, encouragements, appreciations, apologies, informal invitations and replies, and thank-you notes for business lunches, material sent through the mail, or educational seminars.

A telephone call interrupts someone's day. Written notes are lasting, and they can be circulated when it is appropriate. Send a thank-you note or letter after a telephone conversation within twenty-four to forty-eight hours.

Use only black or navy blue ink for anything handwritten—notes, signatures, and letters. Personal stationery for the individual in business must be of quality stock.

Use correspondence cards (approx. 4 $\frac{1}{2}$" X 6 $\frac{1}{2}$") with an envelope, or foldover notes for thank-you and condolence messages. These should include no irrelevant information. Write another note or letter to convey newsy information.

When using foldover notes:

- Do not write on the outside if there is a design or an imprint
- Do not write on the inside top half if there is an indentation from the front side, or if the writing on the inside top half will be legible through the paper or through the envelope when it is ready to mail.

Most notes may be handwritten, but cover letters and a thank-you letter after a job interview should be typed.

It is permissible to write personal notes on a corporate letterhead, but it is always better to type on a letterhead and to write with a pen on a card or foldover note, each of which should be sent in an envelope.

Occasions for Notes

Congratulations. Express your congratulations to an individual for a promotion, for starting a new job, for an exceptional effort, for an important milestone or anniversary, or for personal achievements such as a birth, a marriage, or an honor received.

Thank-yous. It is appropriate to thank individuals for any of the following: for any favor, after a job interview (if typing is impractical), after signing a big contract, or after many types of sales meetings. It is good business to write a thank-you note or letter even if you didn't get the job or the contract. You can thank the individual for his or her time and any possible future consideration.

Apologies. These are most effective as a follow-up to apologies made over the phone or in person. Admit your mistake, express your regrets, and say how you plan to correct the error. The sooner an apology is issued, the more effective it is. Make an apology brief and to the point, not full of excuses for the error.

Before writing an apology, check with the company's legal department about any potential liability your apology might generate.

Invitations. Business invitations may be handwritten, printed, engraved, or thermographically printed. Address and stamp the envelopes by hand. Don't meter them. Invitations should include these six points:

- date
- time
- location with address (map if needed)
- event—the kind of party or the theme for the party
- appropriate attire: casual, business casual, business attire, or black tie.
- how to reply and to whom (see page 269 for R.S.V.P.).

Condolence. When you were the friend or associate of the deceased, or when you know a survivor, a condolence note is in order. Comment on either your respect and admiration for the deceased or your sympathy for the family—depending on whether you knew the deceased better or the survivors better.

Avoid being too personal or sentimental. If your relationship was social as well as business, use personal stationery rather than a company letterhead. *Do not* fax a condolence note. Simply express your sorrow for their loss; nothing we can suggest will assuage their grief.

Holiday Cards. Mail holiday cards anytime after Thanksgiving. It is often wiser to send seasonal greetings rather than religious cards unless you know the spiritual persuasion of the recipient. Many calendars designate most holidays—Christian and otherwise. Sign your name and write a few personal remarks if you wish.

- Personally signed greeting cards always give a better impression. Sign both your first and last names to make sure the recipient knows which *Bill* is writing. Don't make someone guess.
- Signing the husband's and wife's names has created a controversy for years. Should it be *Mary and Joe Palmer* or *Joe and*

Mary Palmer? The rule once stated that a man's first and last name should not be separated. Therefore, *Mary and Joe Palmer* was correct. Today, if one name is better known to the recipient than the other, that name appears first. If the two are known as a couple, the "signer" may prefer to list his or her name last out of courtesy to the partner, but it is not required. Some people feel that the person signing the card for the couple should write his or her name first. The most important rule remains—always include a last name.

- You may send Christmas greetings containing Christian connotations, such as a manger scene, to Christian friends.
- Send a Hanukkah card to a Jewish friend or business contact.
- Send a "Seasons Greetings" card to Arab or Muslim clients.
- You may send company holiday cards to close business acquaintances who know other members of your family. Sign "Katherine Sample and her family," if she is the one better known by the recipients. It is usually inappropriate to send snapshots or family pictures in company holiday cards.

Business Announcements

Business announcements should be printed or engraved on high-quality paper. They can be formal or informal, depending on the type of business. For example, the relocation of a medical practice is usually more formally announced than perhaps a day-care center.

The following occasions are appropriate reasons to send announcements: changing an address, opening a new branch office, changing the company logo or name, adding new staff members, adding a new department, announcing promotions, or announcing mergers or acquisitions.

Addressing Envelopes

> "To address others properly is not only a question of courtesy, but also of a well-polished company image, continued good business relationships, and profitability."[1]

Use of Titles

- Always use a title before or after the name unless the sex and the title are unknown. For example, Shannon Ryan may have a title unknown to you. The sex of Shannon Ryan is unclear. Use the full name, Shannon Ryan, on the envelope and in the salutation of the letter: Dear Shannon Ryan.
- Use only one title per person, per line in an address. For instance, Allen Framer, M.D. (not Dr. Allen Framer, M.D.). Other examples:

  Alice Waller, R.N. (not Ms. Alice Waller, R.N.)

  Mark Allen, Ph.D. (not Dr. Mark Allen, Ph.D.)

  President Carl Wynn (not President (or Mr.) Carl Wynn, Ph.D.)

  Marcia Day, Esq. (not Ms. Marcia Day, Esq.)

Correct:	Mr. Paul Mears
	President, Caldwell Engineering Firm
	Street address
	City, state, zip code
	Carl Wynn, Ph.D.
	President, Browning University
	Address

Note: "Jr." is not considered a title, but part of the name. When Bryant Sims has a son, he may be named Bryant Sims, Jr. (not II). The father becomes Bryant Sims, Sr. When Bryant Sims, Jr., has a son, he may be named Bryant Sims, III. When Bryant Sims, Sr., dies, Bryant Sims, Jr. usually drops the "Jr."

If a child is named for an uncle or grandfather, the young boy becomes the "II." For instance, Ed Snell has a nephew (or grandson) bearing his name. The young boy becomes Ed Snell, II. When the uncle or grandfather dies, the younger Ed Snell usually drops the "II."

Married Couples

- Esq. is never used when writing to a couple, either of which is a lawyer. It is Mr. and Mrs. Miles Day (not Mr. and Mrs. Miles Day, Esq.)

- When the wife has a professional title and he does not:
  Mr. Michael Bartholamew
  　　and Dr. Elizabeth Bartholamew
  Their address

- When both are doctors:
  The Doctors Jones
  Their address
  　　or
  Dr. Ray Jones
  　　and Dr. Emily Jones (or Smith)
  Their address

- When the wife uses a different last name:
  Mr. Clarence Lafayette Millersporter
  　　and Ms. Abigal Bittle Lynnablesmyth
  　　or
  Mr. Clark Mills and Ms. Agnes Ables
  Their address

Socially, a widow retains her husband's name for life or until she remarries. Correspondence to her should continue to be addressed to Mrs. Roger Ventura. She does not become Ms. Emma Ventura, as she would if she were divorced. The divorcee's signature is Marcy Darwick or (Ms.) Marcy Darwick. Address an envelope to her using Ms. Marcy Darwick.

Unmarrieds at the Same Address

- The "and" connecting the names of two adults is reserved for married couples. Unmarried people with the same address are listed in alphabetical order and on consecutive lines without "and" connecting them.

        Ms. Arlis Lane
        Ms. Virginia Lyons
        Address

In such cases, it is actually preferred that separate pieces of correspondence (even if duplicated) be sent to one address.

Other Titles

- The abbreviation for the French word *messieurs* is "messrs." It is used as a title for two or more brothers. For instance, if three brothers own a construction company, the envelope may be sent to The Messrs. Wellons.
- Address an envelope to a young man under nine years old with Master David Anthony. From nine to eighteen he is simply David Anthony. After eighteen he becomes Mr. David Anthony.
- For a young lady up to her ninth birthday, address an envelope Little Miss Susan Applewhite. From age nine to twenty-five use Miss before her name. After age twenty-five use "Ms." unless she prefers Miss Susan Applewhite.

- "The Honorable" is a title of respect for men and women who hold or have held a high office, whether at the city, state, or federal level. It is a title bestowed on another person. The holder of such a title never uses it when referring to himself or herself.

"The Honorable" is used before the given name: The Honorable Sarah Parsons. If she remarries and changes her last name, she becomes The Honorable Sarah Byars.

In ambiguous situations, we may use "The Honorable" in much the same way we use "Madam" when we can't remember the name of a woman from another country. "The Honorable" may be used when we are unable to determine someone's specific title.

Correspondence Faux Pas

- Presuming the use of first names in the salutation
- Responding later than promised, or not at all
- Writing more than one page for the cover letter
- Not using a professional-looking envelope
- Misspellings, "white-out" corrections, grammatical errors, typos, cross-outs, or soiled paper all show little regard for the recipient.

Interoffice Memos

Correspondence among staff members should be short, but clear in subject matter, requests, and any results the writer expects. A memorandum reveals your writing ability, your management style, and even your personality. If you do not know the name of the person in a particular position, you may send the memo to "Attn: (section or department) Re: (the subject to be discussed)."

Because memos are brief, they must include the following:
- who is to do what
- what should occur
- the starting date and/or deadline for action

Don't use memos to avoid face-to-face contact with an individual.

Because memos are for in-house use only, they may include a touch of clean, good-natured humor.

Memos should be brief and give "I would appreciate your tending to this matter as soon as possible." Thank-yous and praise are appropriate also.

Unless a face-to-face meeting is highly improbable, criticism is best left for face-to-face contact. Criticism in writing is more difficult for the individual to accept.

Electronic Communications

E-Mail

E-mail is short for electronic mail, a one-to-one communications service for computer users. One-to-one communication means having a dialog with another person via our computers. We type a few words on our computer, which has a modem that transmits the message over telephone lines to the recipient's computer or other computer equipment. E-mail may be retrieved later by the addressee.

"There are currently 8.6 million E-mail boxes in use, making it a $5.4-million-a-year industry," according to *EMMS*, a periodical on electronic mail and micro systems. ". . . well over half a million small and midsized companies use the technology."[2]

- E-mail offers no privacy. Even the signature block is there for all to read. In some states, E-mail messages are admitted as evidence in the courtroom.
- DO NOT SHOUT IN E-MAIL OR OVER THE INTERNET. Writing messages in all caps shouts to the reader. To emphasize a word enclose it in stars—*...*.
- The E-mail writer can communicate feelings or emotions by using emoticons (symbols). For example :-) may look like only a colon, dash, and parenthesis sign, but in computer talk this combination of key strokes represent a smile. Look at them sideways and you see eyes, nose, and mouth.

The following list includes the most commonly used emoticons:

> :-) smile
> :> grin
> :D or :-D laughing
> :(sad face
> :/ disappointment or skepticism
> :| boredom, or indifference
> >:(anger or annoyance
> :o mild surprise ("uh oh!")
> =:o greater surprise
> 8-) means the writer wears glasses
> :-0 shows surprise
> ;-) means the writer is winking
> :-(shows the writer is frowning

- Computers transmit E-mail instantaneously. Double-check the TO: and CC: address lines because once you send the message, it cannot be erased. Be careful what you say and to whom you send your message.

- Flame mail consists of personal insults or expressions of strong opinion. The E-mail user should write only what he or she would say to the person face-to-face. Impulsive, reactive E-mail users rudely produce flame mail.
- E-mail is often sent hurriedly and carelessly, but users should take a few minutes to check spelling, grammar, and punctuation. Speed does not excuse sloppy communication skills.
- Users should be succinct and informative when writing the subject line. Writing "Important" on everything diminishes its meaning.
- Carefully editing your E-mail messages is necessary to insure that the receiver reads and understands it so they can act upon it. Business people have little time for wordy, padded communication.
- The term *spamming* describes unwanted, irrelevant messages. *Spamming* comes from the name of the canned meat product, Spam, which is a hodgepodge of many different meats. Business E-mail is not the proper avenue for airing personal views and opinions that are not related to the current business issue. It wastes time and space and is usually not useful.
- Knowing the common abbreviations for commonly used phrases can save time. IMHO stands for "in my humble opinion." BTW means "by the way." FWIW says "for what it's worth." RTM means "read the manual." LOL is "laughing out loud."
- To reduce crowded disk space we should delete outdated messages on a regular basis. Keeping only the E-mail messages we need helps us and our network work more efficiently.[3]

The Internet

The Internet is a communications service to which we can subscribe. Today, users of the Internet include many people who are new to the networking system and may be unfamiliar with the necessary guidelines for proper behavior.

- No matter who supplies the Internet access—an Internet service provider, a university, or a corporation—these organizations have regulations about ownership of mail and files and what is proper to send. Ask about the rules if you are not instructed prior to using it.
- Laws about the ownership of E-mail vary from place to place.
- Send only E-mail messages that you would freely put on a postcard for anyone to see.
- Respect the copyright on materials you use. Laws vary from country to country.
- Never send chain letters; they are forbidden on the Internet. A violation can get network privileges revoked. Notify a local system administrator if you receive one.
- Don't send or respond to "flame" messages, sometimes called hate mail.
- Check all your mail before responding. When you receive a request for help, you may later find a "never mind" message.
- Make sure a message requires your response. You may not be the primary recipient.
- Use a subject heading to reflect the content of the message.
- Include contact information at the end of your message. (Sometimes the header information is lost.) The "sig." or "signature" line at the bottom makes sure the recipient knows

who you are. The "sig." should not exceed four lines. It takes the place of your business card.

- Don't send unsolicited mail asking for information on people whose names you happen to see on a mailing list.
- If your personal discourse will be lengthy, include the word *long* in the subject header. Over one hundred lines is considered *long*. If the recipient is paying for connectivity by the minute, the longer your message, the more you both pay.
- If you are sending a file, it should be no larger than fifty kilobytes.
- It is rude to wander off-topic or point out other people's errors in typing or spelling. If you do not understand the intended message, simply ask for clarification.[4]

Electronic Ethics

Privacy for an E-mail message is extremely doubtful. Therefore, do not send rude remarks or subtle innuendoes about defenseless victims.

Perhaps because sending E-mail is not a face-to-face confrontation, individuals are sometimes tempted to substitute rudeness for good manners.

Remember: Do no harm. Instead, send a compliment if deserved. Ask the following questions before sending E-Mail:

- Is the message clear, containing no double meanings?
- Is the wording tasteful?
- Is correct grammar and spelling used?
- Have I included encouragement or a pat on the back when appropriate?

EXAMPLES OF CORRESPONDENCE

A. Business letter with a heading

Associated Products, Inc.

1143 State Street

Anytown, Anystate, 70000

January 2, 2000

Ms. Samantha Ulmstrom
1122 Elm Avenue
Texoma, Tennessee 50000

Dear Ms. Ulmstrom:

Thank you for your letter inquiring into the availability of our products in your area. We are sending information about our delivery schedule and a cost sheet, as you requested.

Please review the enclosed material to determine if it meets your needs. I look forward to discussing how we can best serve your organization.

If additional information is needed, please let me know. We will be happy to work with you any way we can.

Sincerely,

John Stalneker
Director of Sales

c: (the mutual contact)

From the date to the signature block, a business letter may also be written with every entry flush with the left margin. The letterhead and logo may be printed across the top.

B. Example of a business announcement

(Corporate Logo)

The Board of Directors

of

Community Relations

Is Pleased to Announce

the Appointment of

Helga Brainer

as

Chairman for the Bicentennial

C. Note of congratulations (handwritten)

Dear George,

Congratulations on your promotion to National Sales Director for the XYZ Corporation. It was nice to see the announcement in a prominent place in our local newspaper.

I am pleased but not surprised at seeing your success in such a short time.

Sincerely,

(Date)   (Signature of first and last names)

D. Hospitality note (handwritten)

Sometimes called a bread-and-butter note, it should be addressed to the hostess, even if the host invited you (unless the host lives alone). You should mention the host's name in the note. Mail it within a few days after leaving.

The same type note can be sent after a dinner party.

Dear Marcia,

Your hospitality made my visit to your home one I will long remember. The welcoming party you and Ken gave for me on Friday evening was a delight.

Thank you so much for a wonderful weekend.

Sincerely,

(Date)   (Signature of first and last names)

E. A thank-you note for a gift (handwritten)

This type note should be mailed within a week, if possible, after receiving the gift. Identify the gift and say how you plan to use it. A thank-you note is in order whether the gift is passed to you face-to-face or sent in the mail. A verbal thank-you is not enough for most circumstances.

Dear Janice and Mark,

Thank you for the beautiful painting you selected for the fifth anniversary of our business operation.

You chose just the proper size and color theme for our entry. It hangs there now, for all to see.

All of us at Allied appreciate your thoughtfulness.

Sincerely,

(Date)   (Signature of first and last names)

For a gift that comes from a very large group, you may write a thank-you note that can be read to the entire group.

Dear Friends:

Bob and I sincerely appreciate your remembering us on our special day with the beautiful set of bone china. We shall always be proud to use it and will think of you as we do.

We want to thank each one of you.

Sincerely,

(Date)   (Signature of first and last names)

For a gift that comes from a group of three or four, write each one individually.

F. Congratulations on a new baby

Newly born baby

Write a "New Baby" note after receiving a birth announcement. Parents of a "less-than-perfect newborn" appreciate a kind note also. The message should be sent with love and best wishes, just as you would congratulate the parents of a "perfect" baby.

Dear Mary,

How thrilled we were to receive the announcement of the arrival of your daughter! I know you and John are excited about the birth of your first child.

Jack and I are pleased to hear that you and the baby are doing well. We can hardly wait to see all of you.

Affectionately,

(Date)   (Signature of first and last names)

Newly adopted baby

Dear Amy,

Your wonderful announcement came today. Your little Brian is blessed to come into a home such as yours.

Bring him by to see me as soon as you can. I am anxious to hold him.

Love,

(Date)   Aunt Martha

If there is more than one Aunt Martha in the family, she would sign the note Aunt Martha (Woodward).

G. Letter of apology (handwritten)

This note should be written even after a telephone or face-to-face apology.

Dear Melton,

Please accept my sincere apology for postponing our luncheon on Friday on short notice.

About two hours before our meeting time, I received a call from my youngest child's teacher saying that he was ill. Making a mad dash to the school, I learned it was not serious, but required immediate attention.

If you have an open date in your schedule next week, I would like for you to be my guest at lunch. I will call you soon.

I regret any inconvenience my cancellation may have caused you.

Sincerely,

(Date)   (Signature of first and last names)

H. A letter of introduction (handwritten)

Dear Emily,

I would like to introduce a longtime friend of ours, Pam Joiner. She has just moved to our city and is looking for a white water rafter enthusiast. With your experience and interest in canoeing, you could put her in touch with all the best opportunities, I am sure.

I will appreciate any time and help you can give to her in pursuing her hobby.

Sincerely,

(Date)   (Signature of first and last names)

I. A note of condolence or sympathy (handwritten on nice paper)

Compose a note with the bereaved person in mind. If you knew the deceased, mention a quality or a joyous occasion with him or her that you remember. If you know only the bereaved, express sorrow for his or her loss.

Dear Albert,

I want to tell you how sorry I am to learn of the death of your father. It was not my good fortune to meet Mr. Smithers, but I have heard much about the good reputation he enjoyed.

I would like to help in any way I can during this difficult time. Please let me know.

Sincerely,

(Date)   (Signature of first and last names)

The condolence letter or note is understandably the most difficult to write. Many people postpone or do not write one for that reason. To ignore someone's death, no matter the circumstances, is a breach of proper etiquette, not to mention added sorrow for the bereaved.

The following is a very general, but sufficient, note that can be adapted in the event of almost any bereavement. You can add names and personal feelings as you wish.

Dear _____,

Please accept my sympathy at this sad time. I was shocked to hear the news about the loss of your _____.

My thoughts and prayers are with you during these difficult days.

Sincerely,

(or With deepest sympathy)

(Date)   (Signature of first and last names)

Some suggestions on remarks that are *not* kind to include:

- "Time heals all wounds."
- "It is all for the best."
- "I know what you are going through."
- "It was a blessing." (We cannot decide that for the bereaved, even if the death comes after a long and difficult illness.)
- "My own mother died when I was twenty. You are fortunate to have had your mother longer." (The bereaved is understandably not interested in our losses, especially in comparison to theirs.)

In the event of a very tragic and sudden death, avoid flowery imagery describing your feelings of shock and horror. A few sincere words offer more comfort. The length of your note or letter is less important than your expression of sorrow.

Dear Milly,

Please know that Kevin and I have you in our thoughts and prayers at this difficult time.

Love to all,

(Date)   (Signature of first and last names)

No matter how difficult, we should also write a condolence note at the following times:

- The death of an infant or young child
- A miscarriage
- A suicide or suspected suicide. (Don't mention the cause of death.)

J. Acknowledging letters of condolence

Notes, letters, cards, and flowers should be acknowledged within two months. If there are hundreds to answer, you may properly use the standard form furnished by the mortuary.

It says, "The family of _____ acknowledges with gratitude your kind expression of sympathy." If possible, add a few handwritten words of thanks on each card.

If you can write your own personal notes here is a sample:

Dear Norman,

Your message of sympathy (or flowers) means so much to me after losing my dear _____. It helps to know I have you for a devoted friend to comfort me.

Sincerely,

(or Warmly)

(Signature of first and last names)

(Date)

BUSINESS CARD PROTOCOL

- Do remember that your business card is a printed visual image of you/the company.

- Do keep your card easily accessible. Never find yourself "digging" around for one.

- Do exchange business cards selectively and in private at a business/social gathering.

- Do offer your card to someone you have just met *only* after getting to know them.

- Do use *only* fresh, clean cards. Plain paper with information is better than a soiled card.

- Do use your card, if you wish, with a gift to a colleague after lining out your printed name and writing it by hand. You may also write a few words on the back of the card.

- Do refrain from presenting your card to individuals in a large group, especially senior executives. Your intent may be interpreted as overzealous.

- Do not present your card during any form of dining while food is present. (Exception: If someone asks for it at that time, you may have no choice but to comply.)

- Do offer your cards to an audience who is listening to your presentation, if you wish.

CHAPTER 11

Business Gifts

The manner of giving is worth more than the gift.
Pierre Corneille

What Is Your EQ? Business Gift Giving

1. What makes an appropriate business gift?

2. Can a tax deduction be taken for the purchase of a business gift? If so, how much?

3. When is gift giving inappropriate in business?

4. When is it inappropriate to accept a gift, and how is it done graciously?

5. Which employers or supervisors give a holiday gift to their employees?

Giving Gifts to Clients and Customers

Gift giving can and should be one of the nicest customs we enjoy. It is a ceremony as ancient as any we observe. Giving presents began as a ritual to appease the gods.

Today, a gift should please rather than appease the recipient, and it will—when we properly observe the art of gift giving. In business, we give to express appreciation and build goodwill among our associates, customers, and clients. To do that we must choose appropriate presents that are not too personal, but show thoughtfulness and caring. Whether the gift is costly or inexpensive is not as important as the thought that goes into selecting it.

Even in business the thought that goes into the choosing of the gift reveals a company's philosophy of thoughtfulness and caring or one of haphazard selection—just doing what is expected.

In today's technological and automated society, the personal touch can make the difference in how well a gift is received. One of the best ways to put a human touch on a gift continues to be the handwritten note enclosed in an envelope. No matter the expense of the gift, an ostentatious card announcing the name of the company or organization sending the item lacks the warmth that we like to feel when we are on the receiving end.

A business card is not the best choice for a gift card, but it may be enclosed after the owner personalizes it. [We do that by lining out our printed name and writing in our first name or the name we are called, if different from the printed name.]

Even when a company's customer/client list is so long that duplicate gifts must be bought in mass from a mail-order catalog, the donor should plan early enough to prepare a card or personal note that can be included with each gift before the catalog headquarters delivers it.

Occasions for giving to a client or customer in business include weddings, births, promotions, and retirements. We should acknowledge even sad occasions such as a major illness or a personal loss with flowers and a handwritten note.

Some other reasons to give a business-related gift are:
- to thank someone for introducing you to a prospective client.
- to thank someone who hosted a dinner or party in your honor.
- to thank a couple who asked you to dinner at their home.
- to thank someone who gave you tickets to a sporting event or any major entertainment.
- to thank someone who volunteered to help you with a project.

Matching the Gift to the Person

If you are fortunate enough to forego ordering and giving gifts in mass, you should shop for something related to the recipient's hobby or special interest. It's fun to receive something special that we might not buy for ourselves.

The selection is more important than the price tag, but selecting the right business gift is not always easy. Whether it is for a client, colleague, or a coworker, we must try to match the gift, the recipient, and the occasion.

Ideas include a special book or a distinctive bookmark for an avid reader; a silver or gold pen, or an appointment book for the busy professional; an engraved key ring; an odometer for workouts; or personalized golf or tennis balls for the outdoor type.

Other suggestions are a photo album, a picture frame, engraved stationery, a framed print, travel items, luggage tags, an address book, a leather portfolio, or a business card case.

Sometimes we have no clear information about the likes, dislikes, or special interests of the individual. For those times we select something more general, such as a small piece of crystal, a basket of fruit, gourmet foods, or imported teas and coffees. It is wise to ask if the individual is allergic to flowers or the gift you are considering.

If you are unsure about the person's taste, you may ask someone close to the recipient. You can always give something disposable, such as flowers, plants, fruit, or other food.

Gifts for customers and clients should reflect a good corporate image. Most people do not appreciate gag or practical-joke gifts, unless the person is a close personal friend. Even then, the gift must be in good taste. You never know who may see it.

Reflecting the Corporate Image

Suggestions for clients or customers include a crystal vase or paperweight, a quality engraved nameplate, or perhaps a basket of goodies. In the United States, flowers and plants are usually appropriate;

however red roses are reserved for loved ones. If you have any doubts about sending flowers to a man, ask his assistant if he has ever received flowers, or how he feels about receiving them.

Flowers are easy to send anywhere in the world by simply picking up the telephone, but the donor must be careful when giving flowers to individuals whose ethnic background is different from the giver. For diverse cultures we must research the local custom before choosing the flowers. The color of a particular flower or plant may symbolize death or romantic love. The wrong choice of flowers as a business gift can be disastrous.

> An American businessman sent red roses to the wife of a client in Paris. The husband cancelled the contract.

Some General Guidelines

- It is better to choose different gifts for different clients or coworkers on your list than to give the same item to everyone.
- You may want to ask the client's assistant for suggestions.
- You may give products that advertise your business, but they should be useful or practical—and always in good taste. Useless gadgets of poor quality reflect badly on your business or service, especially if they display the company logo.
- For a death, write a handwritten note if possible.
- Impromptu gifts are appropriate if they do not appear to be bribes.
- Wrapping, presentation, and the handwritten enclosure card are as important as the gift. All gifts should be wrapped. Sending an unwrapped gift emphasizes the monetary value and de-emphasizes the sentiment of the gift. Always include a personal note card.

- Keep a record of the gifts you give, the dates you give them, and to whom. You don't want to repeat a choice of presents.
- Gifts may be opened when they are presented unless they are all put aside for opening at a party. Sometimes company policy prohibits the opening of gifts in the office.

Another exception is when an invitation states, "No gifts, please" and someone shows up with present in hand. When such a gift is presented, it should be put aside and opened after the party, followed by a thank-you note or letter.

Declining Gifts

According to company policy or for a more personal reason, we may feel that we should not accept a gift. People often ask, "How do I know if I should accept the gift?"

There are some questions we can ask ourself, such as

- Is the value excessive?
- Would accepting the gift be in violation of company policy?
- Would accepting it put me in an awkward position by making me feel indebted to the giver?
- Is the giver known for trying to buy favor with people?

If we are still in doubt, it is better to decline the gift, especially if we feel the gift could ingratiate us to the giver in any way.

The proper way to decline a gift is to return it within twenty-four hours with a note of thanks. Explain that you cannot accept it.

If you think the gift was intended to be a bribe, report to a superior your receipt of the gift and its return. There is no need to mention the gift when you see the giver again. If the giver contacts you, graciously accept his or her apology (if offered). You may want to repeat the reason you gave in the note for not accepting the gift.

The Thank-you Note

It is better never to assume someone owes us something. All gifts should be acknowledged with a thank-you note. In a few cases, a telephone call is permitted in lieu of the note. Notes should be hand-written, not bought with a printed message. A plain front or one with your name imprinted is better than a note that announces "Thank-you" on the outside.

Avoid clichés. Be as original as possible. Mention the gift by name and why you are pleased with it. If you are not pleased with it, you can thank the giver for his or her original idea or thoughtfulness. Avoid flowery or exaggerated language.

Write on your calendar the date you mail the note and to whom. Sometimes we forget if we actually sent a thank-you or if we just thought about sending it.

Gifts for Staff or Coworkers

In many offices coworkers exchange gifts on special occasions such as holidays and birthdays. Usually these presents are not extravagant or too personal. For weddings and births an office "shower" may be given, or one large gift bought with contributions from the staff.

Unfortunately, gift giving can become so exaggerated that it becomes burdensome. Constant solicitations of coworkers for contributions to buy presents can create less-than-charitable feelings in the office. Workers receiving lower wages than others or those with more family responsibilities may feel unfairly obligated.

Establishing a Policy

Every company, business, or office—large or small—should have a policy regarding the exchanging of gifts within that organization. Every employee should be informed of the policy.

The most severe (and least popular) policy prohibits all gift giving. This option usually comes from the corporate headquarters.

There are numerous other policy options a company can choose.

- One individual or a committee may collect money once a year from each employee. The pooled money is then used for a specific list of occasions, such as birthdays, weddings, funeral remembrances, and get-well cards and flowers. Each individual in the office gets to choose to participate or not. Sometimes management is excluded in collecting for and exchanging gifts because the employer may give a generous annual gift or bonus to each worker.

- Some businesses have a small fund, supplied by management, that provides money for gifts, flowers, or cards for special occasions. Individuals in the office who wish to do so may sign the card accompanying the remembrance.

- Often there is one worker who enjoys being the "sunshine person." This individual may take a vote among fellow employees to decide on the policy for that group. The "sunshine person" selects and wraps each gift. This position may be rotated among men as well as women employees.

- For holidays, some employees draw names for gift giving that will be done at an office party for an occasion, such as Christmas or a New Year's celebration. Management or a vote of the workers often sets a monetary limit on gifts purchased for exchange. Some salaries are higher than others.

The lowest paid worker should be considered when this limit is chosen. The workers should not feel compelled to contribute more than they can afford, or at all if they do not wish to participate.

- A committee may collect money and make the appropriate gift selection. Only the people who contribute will sign the card that accompanies the gift.
- If a collection is started for each occasion, a worker may prefer to give a personal gift or card. Perhaps the two coworkers have a closer relationship than the others in the office. The employee simply explains that he or she prefers to give a personal gift. Giving gifts to one's personal friends who happen to be coworkers should be arranged away from the office.

If the policy decided upon eliminates giving gifts within the organization, individual employees may privately acknowledge special occasions at their own discretion. These gifts are presented privately away from the office.

If the majority of the group wants to continue to send joint gifts, then those workers may contribute and sign their names to each gift card.

There should be no hard feelings toward those workers who choose to neither give nor receive gifts within the workplace. If a coworker chooses not to participate in giving gifts, it is customary to assume they prefer not to receive them also. Some religious groups prohibit their members accepting or giving gifts.

Gifts from Employee to Employer

Traditionally, employees do not give gifts to the boss, but often a personal assistant will give one as a gesture of appreciation. The gift should not be extravagant. In other words, it should fit the employee's budget, not the boss's. The gift must not appear to be "apple-polishing." It may be more appropriate to write a thoughtful letter conveying the employee's appreciation.

Other appropriate gestures for an employee toward a superior might be holiday cookies or other homemade goodies.

Gifts That We Should Never Give

- A gift that is considerably more expensive than anyone else's when presents are opened at a party
- A pet, unless parents agree or adults request
- Anything in bad taste (even though it may be humorous)
- Anything that might embarrass the recipient
- A travel gift that is oversize, or fragile
- A substantial gift to a businessperson with whom you are negotiating a deal
- Perfume or cologne
- Candy to someone on a restricted diet
- An item that conflicts with that person's image. Example: a beach towel to a person who sunburns easily
- Perfumed stationery

Most Asked Questions about Gifts

Q. When is giving a gift inappropriate?

A. As a bribe, in the place of a verbal apology, or as a direct response to the receipt of an order or purchase.

Q. What if an individual wants to give a present as a business gesture, but the company does not permit its employees to accept gifts?

A. Do not violate the policy. Instead, take the client and spouse to dinner or the theater if that is permitted. You can always send a personal note of appreciation for business saying you would have preferred sending a gift.

Q. What about the cost of the gift?

A. The IRS allows a twenty-five dollar deduction, but a more expensive gift may be suitable if given from one high-level executive to another.

> The president of the United States cannot accept a personal gift that costs more than one hundred dollars.

Q. What about the delivery of business gifts?

A. The gift with a note may be sent (not delivered personally) to the individual's home, but it can be delivered in person at another location. To personally deliver a business gift to the person's home is not proper unless you are an invited guest and the gift is related to the event.

Q. Are personal items appropriate for business gifts?

A. No. Examples include clothing or any personal care or grooming items.

Q. Should an employer give a holiday gift to employees?

A. According to Elizabeth Post, "It is customary that, in a small department, the supervisor gives gifts to his or her employees at the holidays. They should be of equal value for persons of equal responsibility. . . . In a large department or division, it is not customary or possible to give gifts to all employees, but it is very nice to extend holiday greetings and a handshake before the holidays and a personal wish for a happy and healthy new year. . . . holiday cards may be sent to the homes of your employees, as well."[1]

Letitia Baldrige, in *New Complete Guide to Executive Manners,* says, "What is good for one company may not be good for another." She adds that if profits for the year are down, the executive may send a holiday card in lieu of a gift with an explanation why the employees will not receive a gift at that time.[2]

Q. Is it always necessary to reciprocate with a gift when we receive an unexpected present?

A. No. The present may be a one-time gift thanking you for a special favor or kindness performed during the year. A card explaining the reason for the gift should accompany it.

Q. What about invitations to weddings of business associates that I choose not to attend? Is a gift expected anyway?

A. If you decline an invitation to a wedding or some other celebration, you may buy a gift, but it is not necessary. A personal note wishing happiness for the couple is in order.

Q. Is it proper to take a gift with you to the wedding?

A. Preferably it is delivered to the bride's home beforehand. Donors who know the groom or his family better may send their gift to his home. Often department stores and specialty shops will deliver a wedding present for you. If the store is part of a chain of stores, you can buy the present in one city and have it wrapped and delivered in another.

CHAPTER 12

International
Business Savvy

Good manners are made up of petty sacrifices.
Ralph Waldo Emerson

What Is Your EQ? International Business Protocol

1. What highly offensive gift was retrieved before President John F. Kennedy presented it in India?

2. Showing the sole of your shoe insults which ethnic group?

3. Which common, innocuous hand signal in America is obscene in Europe?

4. In which part of the world should we never clean our plate?

5. What is the proper time and manner in which to present your business card to someone from Japan?

The Importance of Protocol

Countries have almost gone to war over a breach of protocol. Protocol governs rules of diplomacy—proper procedure. During the time of the Korean War, the shape of a table used for negotiations between countries became critical. Who would get to sit in a place of honor? The leaders settled on a round table so they could seat every member equally.

A breach of protocol can yield calamitous results in world affairs. In business, it may mean we lose out on a lucrative business deal. Protocol is not simply where the guest of honor sits or how one serves tea or coffee. It is a framework within which officials of one or more countries conduct diplomatic affairs with one another. It is also the way businesspeople of different cultures interact without offending.

Doing business with foreign nationals has tripled in the last decade. In conducting business, entertaining, socializing, or traveling among people of other cultures, we must do more than practice the Golden Rule. Why? The Golden Rule says, *Do unto others what we would like for them to do for us.* Yet because our traditions are different, doing what would please an American might be terribly offensive to a businessman from another culture.

Someone once coined the term "the Platinum Rule" for dealing with foreign nationals. It tells us to do for them what they would like us to do, regardless of our American traditions. To accommodate their needs, we are not being unpatriotic Americans. We simply are putting our own culture in the best light possible.

This chapter is not a treatise on why cultures differ. It is meant to help create an awareness of and sensitivity to those differences in doing business with people from other countries. An acceptance and understanding of the differences can prevent our embarrassment and failure in cementing business deals. The first lesson might be to avoid the word *foreigner*, no matter what one's ethnic origin. It carries an uncomfortable connotation.

Good manners for Americans means practicing the Platinum Rule, so long as we can do so morally and ethically. The rule works both ways. We always appreciate foreign visitors who speak to us in English. When they do, they are practicing the Platinum Rule by not using the more familiar language of their native country, which would be far easier for them.

When I was in college, the details in a book entitled *The Ugly American,* and a wonderful foreign language professor, Lois Gardner, gave me a new understanding for people who are "different" from Americans. When we learn to care about the difference and needs of people in other cultures, we broaden our perspective and enhance our own patriotic feelings. "Different" might be holding a fork in the left hand and a knife in the right hand, or it might be the way people greet one another—perhaps with an embrace or by rubbing noses. We shake hands, but not every culture follows that tradition.

The Global Economy

Megatrends 2000 by John Nesbitt and Patricia Aburdene alerted us to a coming global economy and the rise of the Pacific rim countries. In the seven or so years since that book, we have seen a trade deficit in the United States. That means we buy more goods from other countries than they buy from us. American business has been compelled to try harder. To meet the challenge of international competition in a global marketplace, an awareness of cultural differences is essential.

Well-mannered Americans allow, without prejudice, for the differences of other cultures. Within our own country we have become "the melting pot" because so many different cultures comprise our society. Common courtesy and pride in being an American means we are confident enough in our American way to accept the traditions of others.

Proper business protocol is not to be confused with popular debate issues such as isolationism, one-world government, free-trade with Mexico, or the "English-only" controversy. Those are political issues, not issues concerning how we treat individuals.

"Unfortunately, we expect people from other countries to act like Americans, and when we unwittingly offend a foreign client by not understanding a cultural difference, it can lead to serious consequences, or a career change," says Dorothea Johnson, a protocol/etiquette consultant in Washington, D.C.[1]

General Tips for Savvy International Relations

Obtain a copy of a "Culturgram" from a travel agency. These helpful information sheets are usually available for the asking. This one-page explanation of the do's and taboo's for each country can provide information as valuable as the product you are hoping to sell to a foreign business.

Here are some general tips that we need to know in socializing or conducting business with internationals, whether in their country or ours. The primary areas in which we can offend are greetings, names, touching, tipping, food, humor, language, gifts, and gestures.

Greetings

Thank-you's with phonetic spellings:
Japanese—Arr-i-gah-toe´
Arabic—Shu´-kran
French—Mare-see´
German—Dahnk´ah
Russian—Spa-see-bow´

Internationals often consider Americans too friendly and too pushy when meeting someone for the first time. While we shake hands, people of other countries embrace, bow, or kiss cheeks. Some ethnic groups like to make eye contact; others do not. Because countries differ, try to find out who should initiate the greeting.

The proper way to greet a Japanese businessperson is to present your business card immediately. Present your card by holding the corners at the top with the index finger and thumb of each hand. The printed side of the card will face the Japanese client in a legible position. He should be able to see your name instantly. (To present your business card to a fellow American in America too early and in an ostentatious manner is a real faux pas.)

Names

Always ask how someone prefers to be addressed. Sometimes first and last names are reversed. (Allen Tate might be Mr. Allen because that is the last name.) Ask about titles. Do not use first names unless you are specifically told to do so.

Touching

Some cultures forbid touching with strangers. Backslapping is always a bad idea. Do not touch the head of someone, even that of a child unless you are certain it is acceptable. It can be demeaning or bad luck depending on the locale.

Tipping

Always ask what is the expected percentage. Overtipping as well as undertipping can be serious. Do not make a public display of tipping.

Food

Travel with a cast-iron stomach and a bottle of anti-diarrheal medication because you need to eat some of everything if you do not wish to offend. One trick is to cut everything you do not recognize into tiny slivers and swallow quickly to avoid the taste.

In China, if you clean your plate or bowl, your hosts will keep refilling it. Serving pork or alcohol to a Middle Eastern businessperson can get your contract canceled.

Humor

Never joke about the food, architecture, or government of a country, even if the locals do. Making ethnic jokes can have serious consequences.

Language

When speaking to an individual who speaks limited English, use words with precise meanings. Our jargon, slang, puns, and buzz words only confuse them. For instance, "ballpark figure," "bottom line," and "It just won't fly" are incomprehensible to internationals.

If possible, learn some of the guest's or host's language, such as please and thank you. To our discredit, Americans don't study many other languages. English is such a common language now throughout the world that we can communicate with our guests or hosts with little effort on our part. Therefore, when we make the effort to use some of their native tongue, we please them a great deal.

Caution: Learn which words misused or mispronounced can be offensive. For instance, the French use *tu* for *you* when speaking informally, but the word *vous* must be used for everyone else. Using *tu* incorrectly is highly offensive to them. (I know. I was once sharply corrected.)

The Japanese do not like the word *no.* The Chinese frown upon the use of the word *clock* because it is a symbol of bad luck.

The English word *bus* refers to an obscene act in Hungary. Use the word *autobus* instead.

Gifts

In a particular culture always learn when, what, to whom, how much, and how a gift should be presented. If you accept a gift, learn when you should open it and what you should say and do afterwards.

Your choice of gifts is critical because some objects have connotations of evil or even death. Some choices insult religious practices. During the John F. Kennedy years in the White House, leather portfolios were sent with him as gifts to the diplomats he was visiting in India. However, their religion is Hindu and they worship the cow. The error was discovered in time to send another type of gift for him to present, and the cowhide portfolios were brought back. Catching that error in time cost taxpayers money, but it prevented a diplomatic nightmare.

Gestures

> Actions speak louder than words and often say all the wrong things.[2]

The use of hand gestures and body language is always risky. For instance, the OK sign we use by making a circle with our thumb and index finger is obscene in many countries.

In Europe, the only acceptable way to wave good-bye or hello is with the palm of the hand turned outward, with only the fingers moving up and down. Waving side to side with our hand and arm can get us into trouble in Greece.

Showing the sole of your shoe to someone from an Arab country is highly offensive.

Awareness of cultural differences is a must if you want to meet the challenge of international competition in our global marketplace. Always learn and respect the customs of your business colleagues.

A dignified and conservative approach will increase your credibility. You will enhance your chances of getting a signed contract when you conduct yourself respectfully and professionally.

CHAPTER 13

Etiquette with the Disabled

*Kindness is a language the deaf can hear
and the blind can see.
(author unknown)*

What Is Your EQ? Doing Business with the Disabled

1. Do you know the current, proper terminology to use with individuals with a disability?
2. Do you know all you need to know about shaking hands with an individual with a disability?
3. Do you know all the comments and questions that are inappropriate with individuals with a disability?
4. Do you know how to assist a person who is visually impaired?
5. Do you know what "never to do" with someone using a walker?

The proper term today for someone who has a disability is "individual with a disability." The former word *handicapped* goes back in English history to when the British crown gave licenses and special caps to disabled veterans of the Boer War so they could beg on the street for a living. (Our phrase "cap in hand" described these needy individuals.) The disabled community requests that we change our phraseology.

The American Disabilities Act mandates that individuals with a disability be given the same access to public and private endeavors that everyone else enjoys. Most individuals with a disability want the same independence and acceptance into society as able-bodied persons.

Relating to the Disabled Individual

Often those of us who are not disabled mean well, but we are not confident about our conduct with persons with a disability. Even with good intentions we may remain indecisive when interacting with people who have guide dogs, are in wheel chairs, or use similar equipment. We find ourselves in a dilemma about when we should offer assistance. We are unsure how our efforts will be perceived—as helpful or patronizing.

Here are a few guidelines based on common courtesy and sensitivity.

Appropriate Phrasing

First, we need to understand the terminology. If we know the reasoning behind a new phrase, we are better able to remember it. Second, put the individual before the disability and use the word "impairment." Avoid terms that suggest negative feelings of dependency, pity, and disease. For instance, "person with epilepsy" is better than "an epileptic," because the focus is on the individual, not the condition.

AVOID	USE
blind girl	girl with a visual impairment
deaf man	man with a hearing impairment
cripple	person with a mobility impairment
someone dying with cancer	someone living with cancer
wheelchair bound	person who uses a wheelchair

Careful phrasing may be difficult at first unless we focus on the individual instead of the impairment. Making the effort will help us afford the same dignity, respect, and courtesy to others that we like for ourselves. To do so, we use common sense politeness and avoid making assumptions about what the person can or cannot do for himself or herself.

Offering to Help

Persons with an impairment make a personal decision about how much assistance they want or need. Some important points to remember include:

- Speak in a normal voice, not one that invokes pity.
- Give the individual the opportunity to accept or decline any assistance. Simply offer or ask if he or she needs or wants help. "Would you like for me to . . .?"
- If your offer to help is accepted, don't assume you know what someone needs. Ask how you can help. This exchange between the two of you affords dignity to him or her. It also shows that you recognize the individual is not totally dependent.
- Avoid appearing to be impatient with the person if he or she declines your offer of assistance and then takes twice as long to accomplish a task.

Proper Greetings

We should be willing to extend our hand in greeting to a person with any limitation, even a person with a prosthesis for a hand, such as a metal hook. If the individual cannot extend a hand or a prosthesis, it is proper for us to make some other physical contact, unless the person with the disability uses body language and withdraws. If he or she appears receptive, we may touch them on the hand, arm, or shoulder.

If the person with the disability is nonresponsive to us, we must remember not to show pity, disgust, or a feeling of rejection.

Inappropriate Questions and Comments

Unless the person with the impairment brings up the subject, don't ask or comment on the disability. Questions about the person's impairment have no redeeming value. They are simply an attempt to satisfy the able-bodied person's curiosity. Don't ask:

"Were you born with this condition?"

"What happened to you?"

"How long have you had it?"

"What caused your accident?"

"Whose fault was it?"

Certain comments can be as unkind as questions. Don't tell about someone you know in a more advanced stage of the same disability. Don't tell about someone who has the same condition, but with greater problems to deal with on a daily basis. Don't tell about the heroics of someone else with a disability. Don't tell how much longer someone lived than expected.

Concentrate on other aspects of the individual. Talk to him or her as you would an able-bodied person. Many people with disabilities work and enjoy the same meaningful life as others. To build rapport, let the individual set the tone for any discussion.

Specific Tips for Specific Disabilities

Persons with a Hearing Impairment

When you see that a person has a hearing impairment, don't shout at him or her, unless the individual asks you to speak louder. If the individual reads lips, it is important to face him or her, speak slowly, and articulate every word.

Persons with a Visual Impairment

Communicate and interact with the individual who may be visually impaired. If an assistant is present, don't talk to the interpreter as though the person with the visual impairment were not present.

Maintain eye contact and direct your comments to the disabled individual. This shows that you accept the individual without focusing on the disability.

Persons with a Mobility Impairment

If possible, try to seat yourself on the same eye level as that individual. By doing so you will not feel superior and the person with the disability will not feel subservient. You will not be "talking down to" the individual in a patronizing manner.

If an individual uses a walker, never put your hands on it. People who use such equipment can easily lose their balance. A friend of mine sustained a broken leg because someone grasped his walker.

In general, remember to maintain the attitude that the impaired person is no less an individual. People who are impaired will vary in their attitude about their impairment based on their personality, experiences, preferences, and individual circumstances. As able-bodied people, few of us are not impaired to some degree. Ours simply may not be as obvious.[1]

CHAPTER 14

The Etiquette Advantage in Recreation

Steel loses its strength
when it loses its temper.
An old adage

Nothing is so strong as gentleness,
nothing so gentle as strength.
St. Francis

What Is Your EQ? Business Related Recreational or Cultural Events

1. Do you know how to respond when the check comes to your host in a private membership restaurant?

2. Do you know how to return the favor when someone invites you to their country club to discuss business?

3. Do you know the proper etiquette for the golf course?

4. Do you know the proper protocol when the games are over?

5. Do you know the proper etiquette for the tennis court?

A great deal of business takes place on the golf course or in a ringside seat today. Large corporations, small business owners, and people in sales entertain clients at sporting events, either as participants or spectators.

The corporate image is certainly visible at resorts, on the tennis court, the fairway, the racquetball court, and in numerous other recreational activities.

From the chief executive officer to the newest employee, all must know not only the rules of the sport they are playing, but some courtesy and safety rules as well.

A reason stands behind each rule. One important reason for many of the rules is simple courtesy. The Golden Rule is probably the number one rule of the game. Players should do for others what they would like for themselves when their turn comes. Of course, another reason for sports etiquette is safety.

Private clubs and public courses have specific guidelines and laws for their particular needs. You can learn them from the host member if you are a guest at a private club, or you can request a copy of them at public courses.

State and federal licenses and fees are applicable in sports such as hunting and fishing. Know and observe the laws governing the sport or activity in a particular state.

Good Advice for All Sports

Some rules of consideration and safety that players should observe apply to all recreation, whether on the golf course, tennis court, or some other field of play.

- Always arrive on time, early if possible, and ready to play.
- If you have an emergency and must cancel, get another player to take your place.
- When you arrive, greet each player cordially with a handshake and a smile.
- Make certain you know the proper attire for a particular sport or club in the area. The correct shoes are extremely important in sports such as golf and basketball.
- Don't fake knowing how to play the game. You often appear foolish later. Take lessons or read up on the sport.
- Never pretend to be better at any sport than you really are, and don't brag.
- If you are an accomplished player, let others discover your expertise.
- Vulgarities, profanity, and drinking will ruin your image. You may never recover your reputation or the good name of the company you represent. (This applies to hosts and guests alike.)

THE ETIQUETTE ADVANTAGE

- Don't criticize other players, the club, the court, or the surroundings.
- Don't continue to complain about being off your game on a particular day. It becomes tiresome. Don't complain about another player's game.
- Permit only a personal emergency to hold up the game. It is very rude, for instance, to make others wait while you talk on your cell phone.
- Don't play the blame game or portray yourself as a victim when you lose or score badly.
- Don't argue about the score or someone's call.
- Keep your voice at a reasonable pitch for the surroundings. Outbursts of excitement, roaring laughter, and loudmouth joking become annoying. In sports such as fishing, it is critical to remain quiet.
- Bring your own balls and equipment. If you rent or borrow, have them fitted early and ready to use. Remember that many players never lend their equipment to others.
- Bring extra balls.
- If you lose the game because of your partner's poor showing, don't blame or criticize.

Specific Tips for Golf

Public Golf Courses

If you are invited to a public course, pay your own greens fee, caddie fee, or cart fee. If the host refuses to allow you to pay, you will want to return the favor at a later date or find some other way to repay.

Teeing Off in Golf

- If men and women tee off at the same distance, either may start first. The men's tee box is usually farther from the cup than the women's, and the men tee off first.
- After the first hole, the person with the lowest score on the previous hole tees off first.
- Players who are waiting must keep three things in mind: silence, stillness, and distance. They don't want to disturb the concentration of the player in progress. Even another player's shadow can be distracting.
- Slower players should allow others to play through.

On the Fairway

- The player with the ball the greatest distance from the hole hits first.
- All the players should volunteer to help look for a lost ball. The player with the lost ball should not hold up the game for long.
- Players should not take too long to make a shot.
- Players should leave the field of play immediately after their turn.
- Leave the area clean and in the same condition you found it. Don't litter. If you cut up the green, fix it or replace the divot (a small piece of turf or earth dug up by a golf club in making too low a stroke).

On the Golf Green

- First, repair any damage to the surface of the green when your ball hits it. You may need to ask for instructions about the proper way to repair any marks left by your ball or watch others on that particular course.

- If your ball landed away from the green and in a sand trap or bunker, use the rake provided to cover your tracks and leave a smooth surface.
- As on the fairway, the first player to putt is the one whose ball is farthest from the cup.
- If your ball is in the way, offer to replace your ball with a ball marker.
- Offer to tend the pin (a stick with a numbered flag at the top that is placed in a hole to mark it).
- Never step on the imaginary line running between the player's ball and the cup.

Tennis Tips

- Don't cross another court of players to get to your own. Don't retrieve your stray ball from such a court while their ball is in play.
- If a stray ball lands in your court, toss it back as soon as you can without interrupting your game.
- If the tennis net is sagging, secure it at the proper height before leaving.

When the Games Are Over

- Return any used equipment to the designated shelter—croquet balls and mallets, basketballs, or racquetball gear, for instance.
- Always shake hands, congratulate the winners, and thank the players for a good game and for asking you to join them.

Leaving with a positive word will enhance your image and that of your company.

- If you are a guest, you should always write a note of thanks to your host(s). Besides doing the proper thing, you and your company or organization will no doubt be favorably remembered long after the games end.

Private Clubs

Private clubs serve as a member's home away from home. More working people belong to clubs today than ever before. Often they are part of a corporate or business membership. Recreation is as much a part of business today as closing a deal in an executive suite or over a meal in a nice restaurant.

Many companies and corporations sponsor golf tournaments and offer tickets to sporting events to clients, customers, and employees.

Just as strong business relationships are made in restaurants, so are they made on the golf course or some other sports related event.

Usually, the corporate office planners will organize and arrange for such events down to the last detail. The designated host or the guest client or customer may have little to worry about in the planning but may lack confidence in his or her etiquette skills at the event. Here are some tips:

- Anytime you are a guest, carefully observe the rules. For instance, don't require special treatment in the restaurant. Obey all signs such as Do Not Enter or Members Only, unless you are invited.
- Ask your host about the proper dress at the club for a sporting event. If casual attire is appropriate, dress conservatively—no

short shorts or bare midriffs for women or gaudy colored or patterned slacks for men.

- Don't tip anyone such as the coat or locker room attendants or the caddie until you ask your host about the club's policy. You can always contribute to the employee Christmas fund.
- The host will sign for food, beverages, and most or all the services. The guest may repay the host later with a special entertainment.

The Rules for Private Clubs

While the following rules for private clubs may seem stuffy to some of us, we must remember why the lodge, country club, league, or association is called "private." These clubs are supported and governed solely by the membership.

For a guest unaccustomed to the ways of private clubs, an invitation to a sporting or social event can be unnecessarily daunting. With a few tips in mind and a little confidence, we can accept another's generosity with happy anticipation. We may even decide to accept an invitation to join the membership of such a club.

New members in private clubs are sponsored by a member of the club. The board of directors votes on each name submitted for membership. It is inappropriate for a nonmember to ask a casual acquaintance to sponsor him or her.

As a Guest at a Private Club

- If you arrive first, a doorman or some responsible person will greet you. Identify yourself by giving your name and that of the member who invited you.
- Wait in the reception area or the room where you are escorted.

- Do not roam around even if the surroundings are beautiful and you are curious.
- If the host offers, you may accept an invitation to tour the premises.
- Do not order food or beverage, even if it is offered, until your host arrives.

As a Guest at a Private Club Restaurant

- Don't ask about prices (which are usually omitted from the menu).
- When the check comes, don't offer to pay, and don't comment when the host signs the check. Your host will be billed at the end of the month.
- Behave as though you were a guest in your host's home—respectful, but at ease and confident.
- Do not ask your host(s) about membership, dues, or expenses, or compare one club to another.

Reciprocating the Invitation

- If you can reciprocate your host's invitation with one to your own club, do so on a later occasion. Don't apologize if your club does not appear equal in elegance or status. Some call this reverse snobbery because guests may feel embarrassed if we suggest that our club can't compare to their club.
- On the other hand, if you are invited to a club that does not measure up to yours in amenities, it is rude to refuse the invitation.
- If you have no club membership, you can repay your host in another way. Entertainment is usually a better choice than

cash. You may entertain him or her at a public course or a nice restaurant.

- Don't offer or attempt to repay in cash while still on the grounds of the club. If you are a close friend and are invited often, you may privately stick some bills into the member's pocket. Do this off the premises and when no one can observe.

- If your host is part of a corporate membership and the event is solely for the purpose of soliciting or keeping your business, you are not required to pay back in kind; however, you should write a thank-you note.

Hosting an Event at a Friend's Club

Sometimes friends allow nonmembers to use their membership to host an event of their own, such as a business meeting or a wedding reception.

When you use a friend's membership to host your own event, observe the following guidelines.

- Don't ask to use the club unless you know the club welcomes the business.

- Ask only a close friend or business colleague to sponsor your event. Many clubs require the sponsor-member to attend the function.

- If you "borrow" someone's club membership to host an event, keep in mind that you have a serious responsibility. You are responsible for your own and your guests' behavior. Absolutely everything that takes place will reflect on the member who sponsors you. He or she will receive disapproval or even censure for any infractions.

- Gratuities will be added to the bill, which will be sent to your host-sponsor. You should ask him or her the approximate date the bill comes each month so that you can reimburse him or her immediately.
- If you are hosting a party on another's membership, you may want to tip the staff over and above the automatic gratuity charge. Make out a check to the Christmas fund for employees. Most clubs have them. Tell the maitre d' you have done so.
- If your event was successful, ask your host sponsor if you may write a letter to the club's president and mention a few specific details, such as good food and efficient wait staff. The letter will likely be copied and placed in the file of each employee who worked on your party.
- Write your sponsor a thank-you note and reciprocate the favor in some way if possible.

Paying the Bill

Most people want to pay their own way, but sometimes we should graciously accept another's generosity and reciprocate the favor later. In general,

1. Pay your own way when possible;
2. Never make a show of paying for anything;
3. Never argue over who will pay. If one person insists on paying, the two of you can resolve the matter later; and
4. When you are invited to a private club, it is better to reciprocate with a favor than with cash unless your host invites you on a routine basis. If you are the only nonmember in a golf foursome, then cash is appropriate, but reimbursement must be made discreetly.[1]

Patriotism

- Everyone, even the very young, should rise and remain standing during the playing of the "Star Spangled Banner."
- Know the words to the anthem and try to sing. The song is difficult.
- If you are on your way to your seat at a sporting event or at any other public place, and you hear, "O say, can you see?" stop where you are and stand at attention until the end. Be reverent as you would in church or where someone is praying.
- Do not chew gum, smoke, or eat during the singing or playing of the National Anthem.
- When the American flag passes in a parade, stop and stand at attention.
- Men and boys remove their hats. They may place it over their hearts.
- Place your right hand over your heart when saying the Pledge of Allegiance.

Theater, Ballet, and Concerts

"Unruly manners, or ill-timed applause wrong the best speaker or the justest cause." *Alexander Pope*

- The artists are performing live on stage. Arriving late is a major social offense.
- An usher usually leads you to your seats after you hand him or her your ticket. The female follows the usher with the male following behind her.

- If there is no usher, the male walks down the aisle first and stands aside while the female enters.
- If the performance has begun, the usher will wait until there is a pause in the program to seat you. Sometimes the usher does not know the protocol and you must suggest that you and your partner wait.
- Applause is your way of thanking the artists. Applaud at the end of each act in a play. At a concert or a ballet performance, applaud only at special times:
  1) When the concert mistress or master walks on stage and bows to the audience.
  2) When each musical or dance selection is completed. Most musical arrangements have several parts with pauses between. These are called movements, like chapters in a book; therefore, it is imperative to watch the conductor. He will turn and face the audience when the selection is finished and you may applaud.

Etiquette for Certain Foods

I eat my peas with honey—
I've done it all my life.
It makes the peas taste funny
But it keeps them on my knife.

How to Eat the Nearly Impossible from A to Z

Artichokes: Pull one leaf at a time from the heart with your fingers and dip it into the sauce. Place the leaf in your mouth and pull it through your teeth, biting off the soft end. Place the uneaten portion of the leaf on the side of your plate. After eating the leaves, scrape away the thistlelike part in the center with your knife, and eat the heart with knife and fork.

Asparagus: By reputation it is a finger food, but when overcooked use a fork.

Avocado: When filled with salad, use a fork. When served in the shell with salad dressing, use a spoon.

Bacon: When limp, eat it with a fork. When it is dry and crisp, you may use your fingers.

Baked Potato: Do not remove the foil. Make a slit in the top and garnish a small portion at a time with your fork. Don't stir up a gooey mess. Replenish garnishment as needed. When the butter and sour cream are passed, put a dollop onto your plate, transferring it to your potato after you pass the dish to the person on your right.

Bananas: In formal situations, peel the banana, place it on your plate, and cut away one bite at a time with your fork.

Bread or Rolls: Break off a small portion, buttering it over your plate. Finish eating it before you break off another piece. Don't hold flat bread in the flat palm of your hand while you butter it. Loaf bread served on a board is sliced with a knife. You may halve a biscuit or roll, butter it, and eat from that half.

Candy in Frills: Pick up the candy and frills (paper lining) together from the box or plate without pinching to flavor test it. After you have lifted both from the box or tray, take the piece of candy out of the frill to eat it. Discard the paper frill properly.

Caviar: Spread it on a cracker with a knife. Made from fish eggs, caviar is an expensive, salty relish.

Celery, Olives, and Other Relishes: Typically, they are finger foods if no toothpick is provided. You may use a fork, but don't chase an olive around your plate, finally spearing the little escapee. Use a serving spoon or fork to retrieve items from a communal dish.

Cherry Tomatoes: If not served in a salad, they are a finger food. In a salad, cut with a knife or leave them whole to eat. They do squirt if you bite into one, and a bad one can almost send you gagging to the restroom.

Fried Chicken: At a formal dinner it must be eaten with fork and knife. In someone's home, watch the hostess for your cue. At a picnic or fast-food restaurant, you may use your fingers. Tablecloths usually mean that we should eat the chicken with a knife and fork.

Plastic forks and paper plates or boxes call for eating chicken with the fingers.

Clams and Oysters: Spear one with the small shellfish fork (or the smallest fork provided). Eat them whole. When they are served as hors d'oeuvres, on a picnic, or in a clam and oyster bar, pick the shell up in your fingers and let the morsel slide into your mouth.

Corn on the Cob: Because it is never served at formal meals, it may be eaten with the fingers. Butter and season a small portion at a time. Don't eat up and down the row like a mowing machine.

Crab Legs: A cracking instrument for seafood should be provided. After the claws are cracked, the shells are pulled apart with the fingers and the meat is pulled out with the small oyster fork. The meat is dipped into melted butter before eating. The small claws are pulled from the body with the fingers and then put in the mouth with the body end of the claws between the teeth so that the meat can be extracted by chewing. Be careful not to make a sucking noise as you chew on these tasty bits. If no crackers or implements are provided, use your hands. Soft-shell crabs are considered a great delicacy and are eaten with a knife and fork. You may remove the black vein with your knife and fork and lay it on the plate.

Dips: Whether you are dipping chips or raw vegetables into a dip dish, transfer the food to your buffet plate if you have one. If you have only a napkin, hold the napkin under it while you retreat from the communal bowl before placing the chip in your mouth. Never transfer it directly to your mouth from the communal bowl. We must never appear to be eating from the dip dish. Never take a bite from a chip or vegetable and then put it back in the dip mixture to dip it again. Never "fish" around for a submerged chip with your fingers. If fresh vegetables are passed at the table, place them on your bread plate, salad plate, or on the edge of whatever plate you have. Never eat from the serving plate.

Egg Cups: Tap around the top of the egg with a knife. Lift off the top and put it on the serving plate. Season the egg in the cup and eat it from the cup with a spoon.

Finger Bowls: You will sometimes sniff a fragrance or see flower petals floating. Lemon wedges are appropriate in finger bowls only after a lobster feast. If the waiter or hostess brings a finger bowl before dessert, place the spoon to the right and the fork to the left of your plate. Lift the finger bowl and its doily, placing them to the left of your place. The dessert will then be served on the plate. After everyone finishes with dessert, dip your finger tips in the water and dry them on your napkins. If the finger bowl arrives without utensils, it means "use me when everyone has a bowl." Believe it or not, until the nineteenth century it was the custom to rinse out the mouth and spit the water back into the finger bowl.[1]

Fish: Eat baked fish with a fish knife and fish fork if they are available. The rules for fried chicken apply to fried fish.

French Fried Potatoes: The same rules for fried chicken apply.

Garnishes: Parsley, dill, watercress, mint, and other garnishments may be eaten with the fork as part of the dish of food, if you wish.

Grapes: Cut or break off a small bunch from the larger bunch and pluck one grape at a time, thus preserving the beauty of the larger bunch.

Grapefruit: Use a spoon, preferably a serrated one. Do not squeeze the juice into a spoon except at home.

Gravy: Ladle gravy from the gravy boat, don't pour it. If you like bread soaked in gravy, you may put a small piece of bread in the gravy on your plate and eat it with your fork. Long ago, that custom was called "sopping the gravy." People sopped with their fingers and did so only at home.

Hors d'oeuvres: We often call hors d'oeuvres *appetizers.* They have not always been served first. Once they were side dishes.

Iced Tea and Lemon: Cover the lemon wedge with one hand, squeezing it with your other hand. You may choose to put the wedge in your glass and use the iced teaspoon to force the lemon juice out of the lemon in the bottom of the glass, or you may pierce the lemon wedge with your clean fork. If you do not care for lemon, place it on the small dish beneath the iced tea glass or on some other plate in your service. Never leave any garnishment on the rim of any glass.

Lemon and Fish: A lemon squeeze is a lemon wedge wrapped in cheese cloth to prevent squirting juice on someone when you squeeze your lemon. Without a lemon squeeze, use the same method you used with iced tea.

Lobster: Unless the claws have been cracked thoroughly before the lobster is brought to you, you will need a nutcracker. To help pull meat from the claws, use a small seafood fork, to get the large pieces of meat from the large claws and the tail and body cavities. You may use a knife to cut them into bite-sized pieces.

Holding the body of the lobster on the plate with your left hand, twist off the claws with your right hand and lay them on the plate. Again holding the lobster steady, lift up the tail meat with your fork. Cut it into manageable segments with your knife. Using your fork, dip a small bite into melted butter. If the lobster is served cold, dip it in mayonnaise. Break off the small claws and quietly suck out the meat. Crack the big claws and extract small segments of the meat with a seafood fork. Dip that bite and put all of it at once into your mouth. With a seafood fork, pick out the meat in the body. Real lobster lovers unhinge the back and open the body of the lobster to extract the remaining sweet morsels.

Meat: Cut one bite at a time. Otherwise, the food will get cold quickly and the plate will look messy.

Melons: Diced melons and cantaloupes are eaten with a spoon.

Oranges: To peel one, cut several slits in the skin from top to bottom around the orange and peel off each section of skin. Then separate the orange sections, remove the seeds with your fingers, and bite off a small portion of the section of the orange. Whole, unpeeled oranges are not served at a formal meal.

Pickles: Served with a sandwich, pickles are eaten with the fingers. When served with meat, a fork is used.

Pizza: It is informal food fare. Hold a slice with your fingers. Nibble. Don't stuff your mouth.

Salad: You may cut the lettuce with your knife and fork. Afterwards, save your knife by placing it on another plate in front of you, such as your bread plate.

Salt and Pepper: Taste food before seasoning with salt and pepper or risk offending the hostess's culinary skills and appearing to be impulsive and suspicious. Always pass the salt and pepper shakers together. Set them on the table. Don't pass them from your hands to someone else's hands.

Sandwiches: Cold sandwiches are eaten as finger food. Hot ones served in a plate are eaten with knife and fork.

Shish Kebab: Hold the meat-filled spear in one hand and your fork in the other hand against the handle of the spear. As you pull the spear, push the food off with your fork onto your plate. Eat each piece with your fork, cutting it with your knife if necessary.

Shrimp Cocktail: In a tall seafood dish, do not cut the shrimp with a knife. Spearing it with your fork, you may bite into a large shrimp. Cutting it with the edge of your fork is preferable. You may use your left hand to hold the compote steady at the base of the stem. Shrimp cocktail is one of the few foods we can bite from while it is still on the fork.

Sorbet: Served immediately before the entrée to cleanse the pallet. It never contains milk, as sherbet does. Milk coats the mouth.

SORBET RECIPE

By definition, sorbet is a frozen fruit mixture that cleanses the palate in anticipation of the entrée.

2 cups sugar

2 cups water

2 Tablespoons grated lemon rind

$^3/_4$ cup lemon juice unstrained

Set the juice aside. Combine the other ingredients and heat to dissolve. Cool the mixture. Add lemon juice and freeze in small compotes or in an ice cube tray to dish up later. Allow sorbet to thaw slightly for easier eating.

For variations use bananas, strawberries, or limes.

Soup: Soup bowls, cups, and even soup plates should have a plate beneath them. Anytime you put the soup spoon down, always place it on the plate, not in the bowl or cup.

When you have a large, shallow soup plate with a wide rim, you may place the spoon in it rather than on the plate beneath it. The soup spoon handle is low enough to thwart an accident such as bumping the handle and flinging the spoon across the table.

Spaghetti and Sauce: The proper way to eat pasta is to use your fork in your right hand to wind the spaghetti against the inside rim of your plate. Then quickly bring the bite to your mouth, being careful not to slurp up leftover strands. In very casual settings, you may wind the spaghetti around the fork in the bowl of a large spoon held in your left hand. (This is the only exception to the rule stating that a spoon always belongs in the right hand.)

Stewed Fruit: Eat with a spoon. Discreetly deposit any pits into the spoon and back into your bowl.

Tortillas: Tacos are eaten with the fingers. Soft tortillas are eaten with a fork.

Toothpicks in Hors d'oeuvres: Collect them in your paper napkin until you can find a wastebasket or a small plate near the hors d'oeuvres tray for the used picks. Never put them back on the serving platter. Never leave one in your mouth. Toothpicks in club sandwiches should be placed near the edge of your plate before eating the sandwich.

Do's and Don'ts

Below are some important do's and don'ts about food and dining. You will see more do's than don'ts.

You will no doubt agree that some faux pas are so bad they lose something when we couch them in positive terms. The first don't is a good example.

Some Important Don'ts

- Don't ever spit anything out of your mouth.
- Don't stuff your mouth with food.
- Don't reach across the table or in front of others.
- Don't meet your food halfway with a rhythmic "ducking" motion. Bring the food to your mouth, leaning forward only slightly.
- Don't cut up an entire portion of food such as meat. Cut one or two bites at a time.
- Don't push your plate away after you finish eating.
- Don't announce any allergies or dislikes for particular foods. You may discreetly inform the hostess of any allergies to food you may have so that she will know why you do not eat something she serves.
- Don't blow your nose at the table.
- Don't put your used utensil into any communal dish. For instance, don't put your fork into the relish dish, and don't put a wet spoon in the sugar bowl.
- Don't gesture with your silverware as you talk.

- Don't talk with food in your mouth.
- Don't talk about unappetizing or argumentative topics around food. (Politics and religion can generate a heated discussion, which is bad for digestion.)
- Don't scratch, pull at your clothes, or pick at your teeth.

Some Important Do's:

- Do choose only one or two pieces of a food from a dish unless directed otherwise or unless there is a variety.
- Do peel and break or cut up whole fruit when you are seated at a table.
- Do remove a tea bag with your spoon and place it on the saucer beside the cup.
- Do spread jellies and jams with a knife, never a fork.
- Do eat sorbet with the small spoon brought with it. Place it on the plate (not in the sorbet dish) anytime the spoon is not in your hand.
- Do eat seafood such as shrimp cocktail with the fork at the far right of the place setting. It is the only fork you will ever see on the right of your plate.
- Do pass containers with a handle(s) turned toward the intended receiver. Set heavy dishes on the table next to the person on your right or secure it for him to serve himself.
- Do pass dishes counterclockwise (to the right) after you serve yourself.[2] It is not necessary to offer a serving to the person on your right before serving yourself. After the initial pass once around the table, the dish is then passed in either direction, taking the shortest route to the person who needs another serving.
- Do ask the hostess for any item missing from your place setting. "Mrs. Hostess, I seem to be missing a fork."

- Do securely position your fork and knife across the plate when passing it for another serving.
- Do say "Please pass the (dish)." If the dish is very close to you, you may serve yourself. If you do, offer to pass it to anyone else who might need it.
- Do feel free after someone requests a dish near you to say, "You won't mind if I help myself first so that you won't have to send it back this way?"
- Do put any item of food on your plate before eating it, for instance, a roll or a pickle. Put after-dinner mints on your napkin or in the palm of your other hand before popping one into your mouth (to avoid appearing to eat from the bowl).
- Do position the female guest of honor to the right of the host with the male guest of honor on the hostess's right.
- Do cover your mouth with your napkin for a sneeze or an urgent cough. There is usually no time to reach for anything else. Turn your head down and to one side. Avoid sneezing on your neighbor or any food. Afterwards, say "Pardon me."

APPENDIX C

Questions and Answers

The following questions were condensed from my newspaper column.

Q. Is it ever permissible to put my elbows on the table?

A. Yes, but in America doing so is proper only when there is no food on the table. Europeans and most other cultures rest both forearms on the table while they eat. The reason? They hold their knife and fork at all times. We lay our knife down and change the fork to the right hand, resting our left arm in our lap as we eat the bite we have cut.

Q. What if I have to burp?

A. Cover your mouth with your napkin. Try to release the air with your mouth closed. Quietly say, "Pardon me" or "Excuse me." Do not talk about the problem.

Q. What should I do with a dental appliance at meals in public?

A. Remove it before approaching the table, putting it in a pocket, purse, or self-container. If you must remove it at the table, hide your mouth with your napkin while removing it. You might inadvertently throw it away if you put it in a paper napkin.

Q. How do I decline coffee, tea, or any other beverage, including alcohol?

A. Simply say, "No, thank you." You need not make any explanation whatsoever. If the server or others at the table protest and persist, remain assertive, but courteous. No one should ever insist that another diner eat or drink anything nor explain his or her choices. It is not proper to cover the cup or glass with your hand or turn it upside down. The waiter should remove the empty vessel. A hostess will remember your "No, thank you."

Q. Must I eat everything offered at a dinner?

A. It is polite to take a little of everything and eat only what you can without comment. If someone insists, say, "I'm saving room for dessert."

Q. Should I clean my plate or leave a little food?

A. Either way you are using proper dining etiquette; however, refrain from scraping the plate clean or heaping your plate with food you do not plan to eat.

Q. At a church supper or other large gathering, is it necessary to wait until everyone is served before beginning?

A. Usually, the invocation is first in order. After people begin getting their plates, they must wait until five or six people around them have food before beginning. It is not necessary to wait for everyone unless the table is small. You may say, "I'm sure we should begin before the food gets cold."

Q. What do I do with my napkin when I finish and when I must leave the table temporarily.

A. In both cases, "put the napkin on the left side of your place, or if the plates have been removed, (place it) in the center."[3] If you put your napkin in your chair, you may get food on your clothes when you return to your seat.

Q. What if I get something in my mouth I cannot swallow?

A. Hide your mouth with your napkin. Use whichever utensil is in your hand to take out the offending morsel and place the unsightly thing under something like the parsley on your plate. Hide it on your plate because if you put it in your napkin, you may forget about it and drop in onto the floor when you lift your napkin. If you place it under the rim of your plate, it will stare at you when the plate is removed.

Q. What if I drop something onto the tablecloth or spill something?

A. With your knife blade or a clean spoon, retrieve a solid piece of food and place it on the edge of your plate. If it caused a stain or a mess, use your napkin to absorb liquid, apologize to the hostess, and offer to help clean up in any way you can.

Q. What does the term "mind your p's and q's" mean?

A. In any language that admonition means to be careful about what you say and do. One explanation I found reminds us that the letters "p" and "q" look the same except in the distinctive way each is turned. Long ago when type was set by hand, typesetters feared they might reverse the two letters; therefore, they were especially careful with the "p" and the "q". They did not want to offend the reader. We must be careful of the rules of etiquette so that we do not offend others.

Q. How many portions of a main dish should I take when the pieces are small?

A. You may take two after you assess the approximate number in the dish and the number of people dining with you.

Q. Why is it improper to refold a napkin?

A. Presumably to indicate that it is soiled and not to be used by another. Long ago, diners replaced their linen napkin into a napkin ring and used it again at the next meal. (They obviously did not do laundry as often as we do.)

Q. Why is it proper to pass food to the right?

A. When we pass food to the right, we permit the recipient to take it with his left hand and serve himself with his right hand before passing it on. A good etiquette rule of thumb—most things go counterclockwise.

Q. Why must the cutting edge of the knife face the center of the plate?

A. Long ago, as people talked they gestured with their very sharp knives. They made up a rule to always keep the cutting edge toward the diner so as not to cut their neighbor's nose. The rule remains today and is a sign of proper etiquette training.

Q. What does R.S.V.P mean?

A. In French it is Répondez, s'il vous plaît. (Answer, if you please.) On an invitation it means "Reply to this invitation." (If an invitation has "R.S.V. P. regrets only," the invitee must reply only if he or she is unable to attend. Otherwise, an R.S.V.P must be answered.)

Tipping

Bellman: $1.00 per bag. If you require special service, tip an extra $5.00.

Busboy: Tip is not necessary.

Cafeteria: Tip only if a waiter assists by carrying your tray.

Captain/Headwaiter: 5% of the bill if you see a separate box on the bill. 15% is also given to the waiter.

Carwash Attendant: Look for a tipping box. Tip fifty cents to one dollar.

Caterer: The tip is usually included in the service charge. If it is not, 15% of the catering charge is given in one lump sum to the manager to be divided among helpers.

Chambermaid: $1.00 for each night. Place money in an envelope marked "maid" on the last day.

Cloakroom Attendant: Tip $1.00 if there is no fixed charge; otherwise round up to the next dollar.

Complimentary Pick-Up Service: Not necessary unless they help with bags, then $2.00.

Concierge: Tip $5.00 to $20.00 on arrival or $5.00 to $50.00 on departure depending on special services such as air reservations, obtaining choice theatre tickets, dinner reservations at the last minute, etc.

Deliveries: Tip fifty cents to one dollar.

Doorman: Always tip for getting a taxi (fifty cents to one dollar). No need to tip for opening the door.

Fishing/Hunting Guides: $5.00 for 1 day trip. $10.00 for weekend. $20.00 and up for week.

Golf Caddies: 15% to 20% of green fees for 18 holes.

Hair Stylists: Do not tip the owner; otherwise 10% to 15% of bill. Remember the salon's owner at Christmas if she/he is your stylist.

Hospital Staff: Never appropriate, but a gift upon departure to thank a nurse or aide is allowed.

Instructor: Ski, tennis, golf, etc. trainers are not usually tipped. Gifts are proper.

Maître d': $10.00 to $15.00 in a handshake for a good table or if you are a favored regular.

Parking Valet/Attendant: $1.00 to $2.00 in cities. $2.00 to $3.00 in *large* ones.

Room Service Waiter: 15% of bill (even if room service charge is on the tab; that fee goes to the hotel).

Shoe Shine: Fifty cents to one dollar.

Sommelier/Wine Steward: 7% to 15% of the wine bill. Deduct wine cost from dinner bill to figure tip if the wine bill is not presented separately.

Taxi: 15% of fare—minimum tip is fifty cents.

Waiter/Waitress: 15% to 20% of bill. If you are unhappy with the service, reduce the tip to 10% and let them know you were not pleased. Be tactful. If food is poorly prepared, tell the manager.

Washroom Attendant: Usually a coin dish is present. Leave fifty cents. In a luxury hotel, leave $1.00. (Before going to the restroom, be sure you have some change. If not, get some from your escort.)

ENDNOTES

Introduction

1. Nancy Miller Lewis, Gannett News Service, Gannett Company, Inc., *(Little Rock) Arkansas Democrat-Gazette*, 14 April 1989.

2. John Marks, "The American Uncivil Wars," *US News and World Report*, 22 April 1996, 66-72. (Information from a poll conducted by *US News and World Report* and Bozell Worldwide. KRC Research and Consulting Firm polled 1005 adults in February 8-12, 1996.)

3. *Reader's Digest: Family Word Finder* (Pleasantville, New York: Reader's Digest Association, Inc., 1977), 272.

Chapter 1

1. Marks.

2. Editorial, *(Little Rock) Arkansas Democrat-Gazette*, 3 August 1997.

3. Marks.

4. "In Other Words," *(Little Rock) Arkansas Democrat-Gazette*, 3 August 1997.

Chapter 2

1. John Naisbitt and Patricia Aburdene, *Megatrends 2000* (New York: William Morrow & Company, Inc., 1990).

2. Marilyn Pincus and Arlene Connolly, *Mastering Business Etiquette and Protocol* (New York: National Institute of Business Management, Inc., 1991).

3. Chris Nolan and Anna Hunt Chever, *Mastering Business Etiquette and Protocol,* Special Report N107 (Alexandria, Vir., National Institute of Business Management, Inc., 1995).

4. Letitia Baldridge, *Letitia Baldridge's New Complete Guide to Executive Manners* (New York: Rawson Associates, Macmillan Publishing Company, 1993).

5. Nolan and Chever.

6. Baldridge.

7. Jan Yager, *Business Protocol* (New York: John Wiley and Sons, Inc., 1991), 44. Yager did "interviews with top executives as well as a survey of 108 human resources managers nationwide . . . working at a variety of industries and companies throughout the United States."

8. Nolan and Chever.

9. Marjabelle Young Stewart and Marian Faux, *Executive Etiquette* (New York: St. Martin's Press, 1979), 224-225.

10. Louise Fitzgerald, University of Illinois.

11. Linda and Wayne Phillips, *The Concise Guide to Executive Etiquette* (New York: Doubleday, 1990), 188.

12. *Working Woman*, 1988, (n.d.).

13. Ibid.

14. Pincus and Connolly, (n.p.).

15. Nolan and Chever, 31.

16. Mary Ann DeVries, *The Complete Office Handbook* (New York: The New American Library, 1987), 48.

Chapter 3

1. Phillips, 159.

2. Roger Axtell, *Do's and Taboo's Around the World,* The Parker Pen Company (New York: John Wiley & Sons, Inc., 1990), 161.

3. Ibid., 161-163.

4. Clarence L. Barnhart and Robert K. Barnhart, editors, *World Book Dictionary,* A Thorndike-Barnhart Dictionary (Chicago: World Book-Childcraft International, Inc., 1979), 1,661.

5. Ibid., 2,117.

6. Baldridge, 116.

7. Associated Press, *(Little Rock) Arkansas Democrat-Gazette*, July 1997.

8. Barbara Mahany (of *Chicago Tribune*), "Gestures Help You Get to the Gist of Things," *(Little Rock) Arkansas Democrat-Gazette*, 14 August 1997.

9. Ibid.

10. Dianne Hales and Dr. Robert Hales, "Does Your Body-Talk Do You In?" *Parade Magazine*, 12 March 1995.

11. Marilyn Maples, as quoted by Hales.

12. Nancy Austin, *A Passion for Excellence*, as quoted by Hales.

Chapter 4

1. *(Little Rock) Arkansas Democrat-Gazette*, 8 October 1997.

2. *Business Review,* Kwik-Kopy Corporation, May 1991.

3. Company news release, Alltel Communications, Little Rock, Ark., 9 September 1997.

Chapter 5

1. *Today's Office,* June 1986, (n.p.).

2. *Success,* June 1984, 45.

3. Brian Kleiner, "Etiquette for Managers," *Agency Sales,* April 1994, 36-40.

4. *The Economic Press* D, no. 1B.

Chapter 6

1. John T. Molloy, *The New Women's Dress for Success* (New York: A Time Warner Compay, 1996).

2. Dayton Hudson Corporation.

3. Peg Avery and Associated, Inc., *National Etiquette Enterprises Newsletter,* March 1993.

4. Molloy.

5. Ibid.

6. Ibid.

7. Ibid.

8. Ibid., 193.

9. Ibid.

10. *Reader's Digest: Family Word Finder,* 67.

Chapter 8

1. Harriet Aldridge, *(Little Rock) Arkansas Democrat-Gazette,* (n.d.).

Chapter 9

1. Jill Robinson, "Manners," *House and Garden*, November 1978, 184.

2. Nolan and Chever.

3. Ibid.

4. Morey Stettner, *Management Review*, June 1988.

5. *Entrepreneur*, (n.d.).

Chapter 10

1. Baldridge.

2. Jill MacNeice, "Calls by Computer," *Nations Business*, July 1990.

3. *fabrik's E-Mail Netiquette Guide* (San Fransisco: fabrik communications, inc.).

4. *Network Working Group*, S. Hambridge, Intel Corporation, October, 1995.

Chapter 11

1. Elizabeth Post, *Emily Post on Business Etiquette* (New York: Harper and Row, 1990), 34.

2. Baldridge.

Chapter 12

1. Dorothea Johnson, *The Washington Times Capital Life*, 24 July 1987.

2. Axtell, 41.

Chapter 13

1. *National Etiquette Enterprises Newsletter*, March 1993.

Chapter 14

1. Marjabelle Young Stewart, *The New Etiquette* (New York: St. Martin's Press, 1987). Also noted in Letitia Baldridge, *Letitia Baldridge's Complete Guide to Executive Manners* (New York: Rawson Associates, 1984); Letitia Baldridge, *Letitia Baldridge's The New Manners for the '90's* (New York: Rawson Associates, 1990); and Linda and Wayne Phillips, *The Concise Guide to Executive Etiquette* (New York: Doubleday, 1990).

Appendix

1. Margaret Visser, *The Rituals of Dinner* (New York: Grove Weidenfeld, 1991), 287.

2. Elizabeth Post, *Etiquette*, 15th ed. (New York: HarperCollins, 1992).

3. Elizabeth Post, *Emily Post on Etiquette*, 29.

INDEX

ABOUT THE AUTHOR

June Hines Moore has twenty years of experience in teaching and writing about etiquette. She is a member of International Speakers Association, C.L.A.S.S. (Christian Leaders and Speakers Service), and AWSA (Advanced Writers and Speakers Association). For more information on speaking availability, training workshops or fees, you may E-mail June Hines Moore at mooremanners@sbcglobal.net. Specific questions on manners or business etiquette cannot be answered individually but are welcome as research for future projects.

More from June Hines Moore

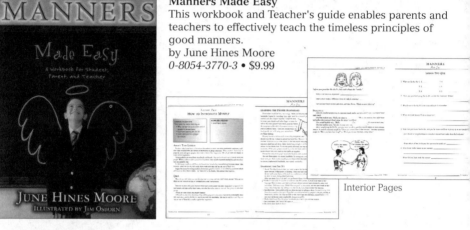
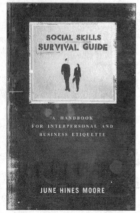